BREAKING
OUT OF
9 TO 5

BREAKING OUT OF 9 TO 5

HOW TO REDESIGN YOUR JOB TO FIT *YOU*

Maria Laqueur
Donna Dickinson

DISCARD

Peterson's
Princeton, New Jersey

Library of Congress Cataloging-in-Publication Data

Laqueur, Maria, 1942–
     Breaking out of 9 to 5 : how to redesign your job to fit you / Maria Laqueur, Donna Dickinson.
       p.   cm.
     Includes bibliographical references and index.
     ISBN 1-56079-351-1 : $12.95
     1. Job hunting. 2. Hours of labor, Flexible. I. Dickinson, Donna, 1958– . II. Title. III. Title: Breaking out of nine to five.
HF5382.7.L356 1994
     650.1—dc20   94-9584
                                          CIP

Text design by CDS Designs

Composition by Peterson's Guides

Printed in the United States of America

10 9 8 7 6 5 4 3 2 1

To Alessandra, Andrew, Julia, and Richard, the next generation.
We hope you'll find the perfect balance when it's your turn.

CONTENTS

Acknowledgments

We have so many people to thank for making this book possible.

We owe a great debt to the men and women who gave generously of their time to share their stories with us and who continually inspired us to keep writing. We are grateful to our friends and colleagues at the Association of Part-Time Professionals who encouraged us to press forward. And a very special thanks goes to Jean White, Judith McVerry, Shannon Hamm, Rebecca Kline, and Kathleen Hindle for keeping our thinking and writing focused and giving us a boost whenever we needed one most.

We are especially grateful to Kathy Fowler at U S WEST, Kathy Zanowic at Bell Atlantic, Sue Pervi at the Catholic University of America, and so many others in the private and public sector for offering us the employer perspective on flexible scheduling. A special thanks to Robert C. Webster of Lawsmiths and Barbara Miller of Allied Health Professionals for sharing their insights and expertise with us for chapter 10.

Finally, we are most appreciative to our editor, Carol Hupping, who believed in us from the beginning and whose enthusiasm for this project never waned.

—M. L. and D. D.

From Maria:

This book could not have been completed without the help and support of my family, friends, and colleagues. A heartfelt thanks to my two sisters, Katherine and Bernadette, who shared my enthusiasm for this project from the very beginning and whose words of encouragement kept me moving forward.

Special thanks to Ellen Canova and Barbara Geiger-Green, my colleagues at the Association of Part-Time Professionals, for their continued interest and enthusiasm for the project.

To my canine and feline friends, Luppy, Fleur, and Shelly, thanks for their company during the long days and nights at the computer.

And last, my love and appreciation to my husband, Jerry Hamm, for encouraging me from day one to undertake this project. His patience and support made it all possible.

From Donna:

I am indebted to my father, Paul Dickinson, and his wife, Barbara, for their wholehearted support and generous gift of a computer so I could follow my own advice and work on this book from home. My heartfelt thanks to my brother, David Dickinson, for his tremendous encouragement and to my sister, Mary Lev, and her husband, Rick, for their constant support and hours of baby-sitting. Special thanks to my in-laws, Marion and Marvin Breskin, for their interest and many kind words along the way. This acknowledgment would be incomplete without remembering my mother, who was the master of juggling ten things at once.

And finally, my love and gratitude to my husband, Bill Breskin, who convinced me to take on this project and who always reminded me of the light at the end of the tunnel. His good nature and infinite patience are as responsible as anything for the completion of this book.

PART 1

Breaking Tradition

CHAPTER 1

IN PURSUIT OF FLEXIBILITY

There is

only one

success—to be

able to spend

your life in

your own way.

— *Christopher
Morley*

How often have you wished for more time in the day? Work, family, leisure, time alone—all this and more compete for our attention. When it gets to be just too much, something has to give. And since you can't stretch the day beyond 24 hours, there are choices to be made. Work demands are very real and often unrelenting, so family and personal time are usually the first things to go.

We've all learned by now that time is the one thing you can't buy and the one thing you can't replace. If you feel that you've reached the point where you've got to do something to create more of it—for family, for friends, for the business you've always wanted to start, or for the screenplay you've always wanted to write—you're not alone.

What would happen if you could cut back on some of those work demands so that there would be more time in the day for other things? And just how would you go about doing it without quitting your job, without putting your career on hold or even perhaps at risk?

We hear such questions over and over again, from family members, friends, and colleagues we meet in our work with the Association of Part-Time Professionals (APTP). And we heard ourselves asking these same questions when we were faced with needing more time on the home front. The two of us chose flexible career paths for very different reasons, but they have gotten us to the same goal: more time for things outside of work and better balance between our working lives and our personal lives.

You, clearly, have your own reasons for wanting more flexibility in your job, and in this book we'll share with you many different ways to restructure your work life—to break out of the 9-to-5 routine—so you can recapture some of your time for those things that matter most to you.

It's not always easy. Gaining flexibility often involves sacrifice. How do you fit such an arrangement into your long-term goals? Do you run the risk of jeopardizing career advancement by working part-time or adopting a flexible full-time schedule? Will you need to cut expenses if your new situation means a reduced income? These are just a few of the many questions you'll have to ask yourself before attempting to integrate an alternative work arrangement into your life. And answering these questions is just a first step, as you'll discover in the chapters that follow.

WHAT'S BEHIND THE TIME CRUNCH?

Why are we so short on time? Just a few years ago, the forerunners of the information age promised us that technology would loosen the grip our jobs hold over us. Computers, cellular phones, fax machines—all of these would be time-saving tools that would make life easier and give us more personal time. Instead, it sometimes seems that the proliferation of communication technology has simply allowed our jobs to follow us everywhere we go, further blurring the distinction between personal and work time.

Perhaps one of the reasons why time is in short supply in your household is that you're part of a two-career couple. You both must manage somehow to fit home and family needs in around full-time jobs. The number of work/family jugglers like you increases each year. Today almost two-thirds of married couples have both spouses working, compared with only 45 percent in 1975.[1] If you're like many dual-career families, you have children or elderly relatives, both of whom may need a good deal of time and attention. But there are other reasons why you may be looking for extra time. Perhaps you want to go back to school for a degree or to retrain, maybe devote more time to a serious hobby, or do volunteer work.

Recent surveys paint a vivid picture of the stress this time crunch creates. A 1991 CNN-*Time* poll of American workers found 61 percent of respondents agreeing that "earning a living today requires so much effort that it's difficult to enjoy life."[2] The Hilton Hotel Corporation conducted a survey that same year in which more than half of the 1,000 Americans questioned indicated that they would happily forego a day's pay for an extra day off.[3]

And recently released results of the study *The National Study of the Changing Workforce*, conducted by the Families and Work Institute, a New York–based research organization, noted similar worker attitudes. Considered the most comprehensive study ever conducted on the work and personal/family lives of the U. S. work force, it showed that 42 percent of the more than 3,000 men and women surveyed feel "used up" by the end of the workday. And no wonder. The study found that workers in two-career households spend an average of 14.8 hours a day doing their regular work, putting in overtime, commuting, doing chores, and meeting the needs of their children. While they feel a strong commitment to doing their job well, they would like to find better balance between work and their personal life and have more time for themselves, family, and friends.[4]

EMPLOYER RESPONSE

It's studies like these, but most of all pressure from employees themselves, that has sent a loud and clear message to employers to come up with programs to ease the daily stress of balancing work and family responsibilities.

In response to this outcry, a handful of America's larger corporations, including Aetna, IBM, Corning, and Du Pont, took the lead in the 80s by offering employees new options over and above the usual benefits packages of health insurance, vacation and sick leave, and retirement funds. They began investing in programs such as child care and elder care, extended leaves, and an array of other programs designed to meet the needs of their employees. These initiatives became known as work/family or family-friendly programs.

While these programs clearly met the needs of many employees, they did not speak to the majority. More than one company survey revealed that what employees really wanted most were less rigid work schedules to fully integrate work and family needs. Again, employers listened to what their workers were saying. Flexible work arrangements—part-time, job sharing, telecommuting, flextime, and compressed workweek—were soon added to the umbrella of work/family programs.

The 90s are seeing employers go one step further in accommodating an ever-diverse work force. Eager not to look like they're giving preference to working parents and willing to acknowledge that there are many employees who want flexibility on the job for reasons besides family, new programs are cropping up under the rubric of work/life programs. With the emphasis off the family, flexible schedules are slowly becoming more readily available to workers across the board.

But it isn't just employees who have found advantages in flexibility. The need to operate with leaner budgets and smaller staffs and the pressure to do their share to reduce pollution and traffic congestion have caused numerous organizations—from Fortune 500 corporations to small local businesses—to take a closer look at a variety of workplace alternatives.

Evidence that flexibility is gaining ground has been reported in several recent surveys. The Olsten Corporation revealed in its 1991 national survey of major companies that 75 percent of the respondents said they would consider hiring workers who wanted special flexible schedules; compare that to only 33 percent who responded affirmatively five years earlier.[5] And in a survey of 7,500 companies conducted by the Families and Work Institute, 86 percent had plans to develop some version of work/family programs.[6]

Government is doing its share, too. Many state and local governments offer their employees a variety of flexible options. And the federal government has recently restated its commitment to flexibility in Vice President Gore's report on reinventing government, *Creating a Government That Works Better and Costs Less*, released in September 1993.[7]

Employers who have gotten behind these programs are reaping the benefits. They report higher enthusiasm, better performance, and lower absenteeism. They see employees responding to the increased freedom with a new kind of responsibility, and many report better communication with employees who are given work schedule autonomy.

In 1990, the Families and Work Institute conducted a survey with 2,000 employees at Johnson & Johnson facilities when that company introduced work/family benefits, including family leave and flextime. In a follow-up survey two years later, the employees rated their work environments significantly more supportive of personal and family needs. Studies like this one show that real progress is possible in a short period of time, even at one of America's largest companies.[8]

That's the good news. The bad news is that, despite the good intentions of many companies, there is still widespread managerial skepticism about flexible work options. Overcoming resistance to change has been the biggest problem in many workplaces. Two other concerns frequently voiced by reluctant managers include difficulty in managing employees who aren't always present and handling the reaction of employees who aren't eligible or whose jobs are inappropriate for flexible hours.

Despite the relatively good track record small business has in offering flexible schedules—often used to offset lower salaries—they have had a harder time than their larger counterparts in developing equally comprehensive work/family programs. For many, the cost of offering these benefits is prohibitive. But more than one small business has found that flexible schedules are a low-cost way to be responsive to employees' needs.

While these and other concerns have made many organizations slow to adopt flexible work arrangements, we should recognize the progress that has been made. Ellen Galinsky, veteran consultant to corporate America, summed it up aptly when she said, "In 1980 when I began my first work/family research project and people asked me what kind of work I did, my response required a long explanation. The terminology work and family had no name recognition. Twelve years later, there is absolutely no confusion. The statement that I conduct research on work and family life issues usually prompts a personal story of feeling torn by too much to do and not enough time."[9]

WORKER RESPONSE

Employees, while often quick to embrace the concept of flexibility in conversation, feel conflicts as well. Men especially seem to have a hard time taking advantage of family-leave programs, even when those programs are authorized by their employers. A spokesperson at Levi Strauss reports that most women who are eligible for family leave have taken it while "only a few" men have.[10] Similar gender distinctions have been found in other workplaces. Overall, the number of men using flexible work options is still very small.

Many of us want greater freedom to focus on personal life, yet inside we can't shake the puritanical sense of selfless devotion to work that we have become conditioned to throughout the years. The only way to really resolve this conflict is to look both inside yourself and outside of your situation in order to create a plan that will really work for both you and your employer. We all need to feel productive and valuable in our work. Your arrangement should facilitate that mutual satisfaction, not hinder it.

Pat Katepoo is a good example of someone who found a happy medium between work and home life. Working full-time as the director of nutrition for a forty-physician medical group in Hawaii, she began thinking about cutting back to part-time as her wedding drew nearer. Knowing she would need time to adjust to the marriage and her role as parent to her fiance's seven-year-old son, Pat approached her supervisor about reducing her workweek. Despite Pat's good track record, the supervisor felt the job required a full-time person. So Pat worked out an arrangement with a boss who didn't want her to leave.

"I recruited my replacement and created a new position for myself that utilized my experience developing physicians' practices," Pat explains. She worked out a new arrangement: 8:00 a.m. to 2:00 p.m., five days a week, with prorated salary and benefits. This arrangement let the medical group retain a valuable person, while Pat was able to keep a job she loves. It also gave her afternoons free to pick up her stepson at school and enjoy her new parenting responsibilities.

Pat looked at the situation from all sides and addressed it with a creative solution that worked for everyone.

And then there's Bob McLaughlin. A couple of years ago, Bob, a program director with the International Planned Parenthood Organization, decided he wanted to free some of his time to pursue other interests. He and his boss eventually worked out a plan that allowed Bob to cut back his work schedule by 60 percent the first year.

Bob's boss, who had always operated on a face-to-face management philosophy, had some reservations initially. Finally he relented and agreed to give the idea a try. Bob now works on an as-needed basis with a fax and computer link, and he continues to make a strong contribution to the organization. "I've assured my boss that all he has to do is give me a deadline, and I'll meet it in my own way."

Both Pat and Bob constructed well-planned proposals and arguments for the situation they hoped to attain. They recognized that they had to take ownership of their job to prove their new arrangement could work. And like true owners, they delivered.

THIS BOOK IS FOR YOU

You're probably well aware of the difficulty of combining more time for your personal life with the rigors of a demanding job. But we hope that you can already see in just the first few pages of this book some of the possible solutions. As you read on our message will become clear to you: If you want a better balance in your life, you *can* have it. With work and good planning, you can either restructure the job you have now or find yourself a new job with built-in flexibility.

Breaking Out of 9 to 5 is about making decisions, developing strategies, and taking action. In the following chapters we'll look at a number of practical ways to build flexibility into your working situation. We'll examine the benefits of a reduced schedule and a compressed workweek by studying the cases of people who have made it happen, and we'll explore some of the pitfalls they've experienced. We'll look at the advantages and disadvantages of flextime, job sharing, telecommuting, and other alternatives to the 9-to-5 routine. And we'll help you determine the best method for making your dream of more time a reality.

If you're just now familiarizing yourself with flexible work schedules, chapter 2 will give you a detailed look at each of the most popular options. In deciding your best course, refer to chapter 3, which challenges you to assess flexibility against your short- and long-term career plans. Chapter 4 focuses on the cost of flexibility, particularly when it comes to salary and benefits issues.

Many times the best starting point in the search for balance is no further than your own office. Chapters 5, 6, 7, and 8 take you through all the steps of redesigning your current job: how to write a winning proposal, negotiate the best terms, and make your arrangement a success both for you and your employer.

If you're unable to negotiate a viable agreement, or if you're currently unemployed or just ready to make a change, then chapters 9 and 10 will assist you in finding the new flexible job that best suits your needs.

Throughout the book you'll read about the experiences of other people—both employees and their supervisors—who have made it work. All the people you'll read about are real people, and their stories are just as they happened. We use them to explore the many options that are available to you. We know it can work, because job flexibility has worked for us, and we've seen it work for people all over the country and in all occupations. We've gotten support from each other and from the thousands of people who have turned to us for help at the Association of Part-Time Professionals and in turn have helped us write this book.

We wish you the best of luck as you start your own pursuit of flexibility. It's a pursuit that promises great rewards if you're honest with yourself about what you need and what you're willing to give in order to get it. And the best part about it is that what you gain from your own efforts is the one thing no one else can give you: time for what really matters to you.

CHAPTER 2

NEW WAYS TO WORK

We have a

choice: to

plow new

ground or let

the weeds grow.

— *Anonymous*

F lexible work options are like Chinese restaurants. There's something for everyone. Whether you need a full-time income or you can afford to cut back, you've reached the top of your career or you're just starting out, you're part of the management team or on the staff, there's an option on the menu for you.

Your challenge lies in finding the right one. And the choices may be greater than you think. Depending on your personal priorities, career goals, and financial needs, you can stay in your current full-time job but redesign the hours or days you work; you can work all or part of your time at home; you can start over by changing jobs; or you can pursue a new career path.

Flexible work arrangements has become the catch-all term for a variety of work-site options that part from the conventional Monday-through-Friday, full-time workweek. One of the greatest misconceptions about these new ways to work is that they're only for people who want to work part-time. On the contrary, the majority of people who are "flexing" their schedules are working full-time.

The five most common arrangements and the ones we focus on here are: part-time, job sharing, compressed workweek, flextime, and telecommuting. Compressed workweek and flextime let you choose a schedule that suits your needs without sacrificing salary or benefits. Part-time and job sharing offer relief from the 40-hour workweek, freeing you up for family activities, continuing education, volunteer and civic work, professional development, and other personal pursuits. And telecommuting lends itself to either full- or part-time work.

In this chapter we highlight the salient features of each option and offer you a glimpse into how people have made their own flexible arrangements work. You'll see for yourself each option's advantages and disadvantages and how your pay and benefits may be affected. And you'll get some insight into the employer's perspective. All this will provide you with a starting point for pursuing an option that's right for you.

There are two other flexible work options that we don't explore in this chapter. They are working for yourself and temping. Labeled the contingent work force, these people are casual part-timers, consultants, independent contractors, peripherals, leased employees, freelancers, and temporaries. We take a closer look at this emerging group of "independents" in chapter 10.

THE PERMANENT PART-TIME OPTION

Permanent part-time is the oldest of all work options. An arrangement that lets an employee work less than a standard full-time schedule (which is usually 40 hours a week) on a regular basis, it became popular in the mid-70s when women started pursuing steady part-time employment rather than part-time work on a temporary or seasonal basis.

Historically, part-timers were faced with low-paying jobs in retail sales, office work, food service, teaching, and nursing. But times are changing. Today part-time opportunities can be found in a broad spectrum of both blue- and white-collar jobs. Of the 20 million people working part-time, more than 4.5 million are professionals—90 percent of whom work part-time by choice.[1] Still used primarily by women who are balancing work and family needs, it has gained increasing acceptance with students, retirees, and men and women seeking time for other interests.

Effect on Pay and Benefits

Ideally, permanent part-timers should enjoy the same rights and benefits available to full-timers. In reality, that's not always the case. With the exception of federal and state government agencies, treatment of pay and employee benefits for part-timers varies widely from one organization to another.

If you're employed full-time and reduce your hours, your pay will be prorated according to the number of hours you now work. Although your salary may be converted to an hourly wage, you'll have a better chance of receiving equitable pay for the field you're in by staying with your current employer. If you're job hunting, don't be surprised to find salaries for some part-time positions lower than their full-time equivalent. Many employers still operate under the outdated concept that part-timers are less committed and less productive employees than full-time workers.

When it comes to benefits, there is no uniform standard that employers follow. Some give part-timers the same benefits accorded to full-time employees; others extend only partial benefits or none at all. You'll find a more detailed discussion of the effects of working part-time on pay and benefits in chapter 4.

Schedule Variations

Part-time arrangements offer an infinite variety of scheduling possibilities and for this reason mean something different to everyone. To some, it's a two- or three-day workweek; to others, it's working four or five shorter days. However, most part-timers and their employers agree on a set schedule of hours to be worked on a regular basis.

Advantages and Disadvantages

Permanent part-time is an attractive option for the following reasons:

- It offers you the widest range of scheduling possibilities.
- You have more time for being with family, continuing your education, or pursuing other interests.
- You can continue working at your own pace.

But consider the following drawbacks:

- Your employee benefits may be significantly reduced.
- You may find promotions less frequent.
- You may have to give up parts of your job you find rewarding.
- You may be the first to go if there's a layoff.
- It may be hard to find part-time work in your field.
- Job assignments are sometimes more routine and less challenging.

What Employers Think

Although part-time work has been around a long time, employer attitudes are mixed. Some still view part-timers as a peripheral part of the work force. Others recognize them as an integral part—a fact brought out in several recent surveys.

Of the 521 large companies surveyed in 1989 by the Conference Board, a business and economic research organization in New York, 90 percent of them offered part-time arrangements to employees.[2] Another study of 463 employers representing a cross section of industries, conducted by the International Foundation of Employee Benefit Plans, a research organization in Brookfield, Wisconsin, found the trend continuing: More than 80 percent of the study participants extend part-time arrangements to current employees.[3]

The Part-Time Solution
&

Flexibility is the watchword for making Nancy Simioni's part-time schedule work. A senior project engineer at General Motors Corporation in Warren, Michigan, Nancy has worked 24 hours a week for four years. As the first engineer at the company to work part-time, she has blazed a trail for the six other engineers who have followed.

Jim Welton, director of the Mid-Size Interior and Safety Systems Department, is credited with getting behind the company's "flex-service plan" and putting it into action. He supports part-time work arrangements for his engineers because "these employees have a lot of experience that I would hate to see walk away."

Nancy is generally able to stick to her schedule because she and her managers team up to keep the work flowing at the right pace and to adapt to one another's needs. Jim offers management's viewpoint: "We try to be flexible and we expect them to be flexible, too." That flexibility translates into Nancy's being able to change her schedule on short notice for either a work or family need. "If there's a meeting on a day I'm not supposed to come in, I try to make it, and, likewise, if my son is sick, I stay home and work the next day," she explains.

That same practical approach helps to keep Nancy's workload at bay. Since most of the engineers who work part-time keep to a three-day-a-week schedule, they're often assigned to projects where the work isn't as deadline-driven. Jim explains, "It's best to have

(continued on next page)

(continued from previous page)

flex-service employees in jobs where they have control over their schedules. They're normally involved in projects at an earlier part of the design cycle where daily deadlines won't present a problem."

Like many part-timers, technology fits into the efficiency equation, too. Nancy singles out voice mail as an indispensable tool for keeping on top of things in the office on the days she's away.

Even though working part-time offers Nancy many solutions for keeping her personal life in balance, she has felt some side effects on the professional front. Dealing with the threat of layoffs in a fragile automotive market is one of them. "The worst part about working part-time is the lack of job security because part-timers are the first to go during a layoff," she admits.

This became a real issue for Nancy in the spring of 1993. Faced with the threat of being laid off, she reluctantly agreed to work full-time to protect her job. However, when the scare was over four months later, she promptly returned to her part-time schedule. Uneasy about giving in to working full-time but eager to keep her job, Nancy says, "I've pioneered a lot of things for women and don't like to do anything that I think will hurt the people who come behind me, so I had to come to grips with this one."

Nancy has also had to temper her goals for getting ahead in her career but feels she is limited only as long as she works part-time. She said, "When I chose to work part-time, I put myself on the 'mommy track'. But I was relieved when I briefly returned to full-time work in the spring and I soon had several managers offering me other positions in the company with a lot of growth potential." Even though she held fast to her commitment to work part-time and declined the offers, she was encouraged that her extended part-time schedule had not been held against her.

The key to Nancy's success is a desire to make it work on both sides of the desk. Nancy holds up her end of the bargain by delivering what she promises and management holds up its end by being realistic about what can be accomplished on a reduced schedule. Jim said it best: "Flexibility goes both ways."

THE JOB-SHARE OPTION

In a job-share arrangement two people share the duties and responsibilities of one full-time position. Typically, job sharers divide the work up in one of two ways: shared responsibility or divided responsibility.

Partners who jointly share the full range of tasks associated with the job are considered interchangeable, with either team member able to pick up where the other left off.

Those who divide up the responsibilities generally do so according to project, client group, or their respective interests and strengths. At times they may work in a collaborative effort; at other times each works independently.

Traditionally an option used by health care workers and educators, job sharing has become increasingly available to people in a wide range of occupations in both the public and private sectors. Today, it's an option used by many professionals who want to work part-time but are in positions that require full-time coverage.

Effect on Pay and Benefits

Most employers strive to keep salary and benefits equitable between job-share partners, prorating both according to the number of hours each partner works. In some cases, salaries may vary slightly if one partner has been in the job for a longer period of time.

Statutory benefits (i.e., social security, unemployment insurance, and worker's compensation insurance) are automatically prorated. Supplemental benefits such as health insurance and pension plans are treated in a variety of ways, depending on company policy. Some organizations classify job sharers as part-timers and base their benefits on the policy for part-timers. In other organizations the job being shared is treated as a full-time position, entitling job sharers to split one standard benefits package. And employers who offer cafeteria-style benefits make it easier for job sharers to tailor their benefits to their respective needs. For example, one partner may not need health benefits so she or he opts for a child-care subsidy instead.

Job Sharing: Two Workers for the Price of One

Bonnie Steuart and Sallie Reese may as well be joined at the hip. They think alike, finish each other's sentences, and even cook dinner for one another's family one day a week. They are not identical twins; they are job sharers.

Since June 1990, Sallie and Bonnie have shared the job of manager for large business support at Bell Atlantic in Arlington, Virginia. They take pride in working in a way they call "seamless." In other words, everyone they come into contact with has no idea of where the work of one ends and where the work of the other picks up. Instead of dividing their job by project, they choose to share every task so both are up to speed and ready with an answer when their boss, co-workers, or clients call.

Sallie works on Monday, Wednesday, and Friday, which suits her need for variety during the week. And Bonnie's schedule of working long days on Tuesday and Thursday gives her much-coveted four-day weekends at home. Bonnie's share of salary and bonuses is 50 percent to Sallie's 60 percent. They evenly split one benefits package with each paying for half of her health benefits.

Even though this job-share team costs Bell Atlantic about 110 percent of one full-time salary, the company is glad to hang on to two high-performing employees with 21 years of training and experience between them. At the end of the trial period for their job-share arrangement, their supervisor, Donald Carr, said "Bonnie's and Sallie's job-share trial has been an unqualified success. It provides a means to retaining high-quality managers and allows employees to balance their lives. It's been a win-win situation."

Bonnie's and Sallie's conscientious attitude about operating as one employee saves the company money in other ways. Bonnie says, "Since we share one job, we feel it's important to spend corporate

(continued on next page)

(continued from previous page)

money responsibly by keeping our expenses down." They make their point by ordering one set of stationery and business cards with both their names on it. On business trips they always share a room and look for "two-for-one" train and air fares.

Bonnie prefers job sharing to a regular part-time job: "With job sharing you have peace of mind that your work is being done while you're away. I don't spend my days off worrying about the job because I know Sallie is there when something comes up." Sallie agrees: "One of the biggest advantages of job sharing for me is that I don't get burned out on high-stress assignments. By working every other day, I have a fresh perspective on the days that I do work."

The job-share experience has exceeded Bonnie's and Sallie's expectations. As much as they enjoyed working full-time and may return to it once their children are grown, for now this arrangement lets them keep their careers and families on track.

Schedule Variations

Job-share schedules can be designed in a variety of ways, depending on the requirements of the job, the preferences of the supervisor, and the needs of the job-share team. Some job sharers prefer to work partial days every week, others find splitting the week or one-week-on/one-week-off preferable. Hours are not always divided equally. For example, the job split may be 60/40 or even 75/25. In arrangements where assignments are worked on jointly, partners usually build in overlap time. We've also heard of instances in which the partners rotate on a monthly basis, but these are unusual cases. The following are examples of typical schedules:

Split week, consecutive days: Both partners work two 8-hour days and one 4-hour day, with Wednesday the overlap day.

Partner A works 8-hour days Monday, Tuesday, and ½ of Wednesday
Partner B works ½ of Wednesday, and 8-hour days Thursday, Friday

A two/three day split with no overlap: One partner works two 8-hour days per week; the other works three 8-hour days per week.

Partner A works Monday, Tuesday

Partner B works Wednesday, Thursday, Friday

Split week: Partners rotate, working two days one week, three days the second week.

Week 1: Partner A works Monday, Tuesday, Wednesday

Partner B works Thursday, Friday

Week 2: Partner A works Monday, Tuesday

Partner B works Wednesday, Thursday, Friday

Advantages and Disadvantages

Job sharing has become an increasingly popular and practical option for these reasons:

- It offers a good solution if you want to work part-time but your job requires full-time coverage.
- You have a chance to retain seniority and status in your current position.
- You have a chance to perform parts of the job most suited to your skills and abilities.
- You and your partner can use each other as sounding boards, can provide different perspectives, and can offer co-worker support.
- There is potential for reducing burnout if you're in a high-stress job.

The main drawbacks to job sharing are the following:

- You and your partner must rely on one another for success.
- If you turn your full-time job into a job share, you may find it difficult to share the authority and power previously held alone.
- You may experience a loss of job satisfaction if you're unable to see a project through from beginning to end.

Teaming Up with the Right Partner

The key to success of every job-share arrangement is finding a compatible partner. You're off to a good start if you already have someone in mind, perhaps a co-worker or friend who is looking for a part-time job. If you're faced with looking for a partner, survey your co-workers, scan your network of personal contacts, or consider advertising through your own employer or in the newsletter of an appropriate professional association. Keep in mind the following characteristics you and your partner should share to make your arrangement a success:

- commitment to each other and to making the job-share arrangement work
- compatibility in personality, attitude, and work style
- complementary skills, knowledge, and abilities
- excellent communication with each other and with anyone else affected by the arrangement
- willingness to complete a task you did not start or to let your partner take over one you may have initiated

What Employers Think

The job-share concept, around since the 1960s, has only recently been viewed as a feasible alternative by employers. Employee requests for job-share arrangements and the desire of employers to hold on to good employees who want to work part-time have prompted many companies to implement this option. According to a 1991 survey by the Conference Board, a New York–based research organization, more than one-half of the 153 companies surveyed offered job sharing.[4]

As with the part-time and telecommuting options, managers who have had experience with job sharing generally support it enthusiastically. They are aware of the advantages that come from having the skills, experience, and energy of two people in one job. And some encounter the added benefit of having partners fill in for each other when one is sick or on vacation, offering continuity in the job.

Managers who lack experience with job sharing tend to be skeptical and are often reluctant to give it a try. Their reluctance is based on concerns such as the cost of additional benefits and training, the ability of two people to deal effectively with the rest of the staff, clients, and customers, and the void left when one partner leaves.

Despite this reluctance job-share programs are catching on. The airline industry was added recently to the ranks of organizations who've adopted job sharing on a company-wide basis. Responding to employee requests and concerned about keeping well-trained, productive workers, USAir piloted a job-share program at its corporate headquarters in Arlington, Virginia, in late 1992.

According to Pat Chernesky, USAir's employee relations representative, it also turned out to be a morale booster during tough economic times. After a successful trial period, job sharing was opened up to all nonunion employees on a company-wide basis in positions ranging from receptionist to senior analyst.

THE COMPRESSED WORKWEEK
OPTION

A compressed workweek refers to a work schedule in which the standard number of full-time hours—usually 40—are worked in less than five days. It got its start in 1940 when Mobil and Gulf Oil boldly implemented the 10-hour, four-day workweek for their truck drivers. Use of the compressed workweek has been sporadic since then. It enjoyed a brief period of popularity in the 70s and since the early 90s has become a more widely accepted option for both employers and employees.

Effect on Pay and Benefits

There is little, if any, impact on your pay and benefits since you're continuing to work full-time. The one exception may be holidays. Your work schedule, along with company policy, will determine how many and which holidays you get. For example, if you received five paid holidays (8 hours each) when working a regular five-day-a-week schedule, under the four-day, 40-hour scheme, your holiday benefits might be adjusted to four paid holidays (10 hours each). The total number of holiday hours remains the same; it's only the number of days that changes.

Schedule Variations

For the most part, compressed workweek schedules are based on the standard 40-hour workweek. In companies where a 35-to-38-hour workweek is the standard, slight variations may occur. The most common types of compressed workweek schedules are:

- The 4/40 scheme—four consecutive 10-hour days per week (usually Monday through Thursday or Tuesday through Friday) with one day off per week. This is the most widely used schedule because it requires the least amount of adjustment in the workplace.
- The 4½/40 scheme—four 9-hour days plus one 4-hour day with ½ day off per week. This is a schedule used by many employers during the summer months.
- The 9/80 scheme—9-hour days in alternating five-day and four-day weeks. This is a popular option with government agencies.
- The 3/36 scheme—three 12-hour days, with two days off per workweek. Commonly used in hospitals, this scheme is gaining acceptance by a growing number of companies in the service industries.

Advantages and Disadvantages

A compressed workweek won't reduce your work load, but it can offer you the following advantages:

- You would enjoy a regular three- or four-day weekend.
- You would have time off from work without reduction in income and benefits.
- Your commuting time could be reduced if you end up traveling during off-peak hours.
- You would need a reduced number of days per month for dependent care, if that's a concern for you.

As attractive as it may seem, working a compressed work schedule has some significant drawbacks worth considering:

- You may find working 10- or 12-hour days on a regular basis exhausting.
- It may be more difficult to find dependent care for 11 to 13 hours per day (allowing for commuting time).

- You may find state wage and hour legislation restricts the maximum number of hours you can work in one day.

What Employers Think

One of the oldest options, the compressed workweek has received mixed reviews during its fifty-year history. For the most part, employers view it as a low-cost measure to give employees flexibility in balancing their work and nonwork lives. But there are business advantages, too. A compressed workweek schedule can be designed to extend business hours and provide more shift coverage during peak periods.

Despite these advantages, some employers find that the combination of longer workdays and shorter workweeks can cause supervision, communication, and scheduling problems. Nevertheless, a growing number of public and private sector organizations are adding it to their list of available work options. Some examples are the following:

- The Bureau of National Affairs, a publishing company in Washington, D.C., instituted a compressed workweek program in its indexing department that allows employees to condense their workweek into four or four and a half days. Those working four days take either Monday or Friday off. All employees must be in the office for core time, which is Tuesday through Thursday, 10:00 a.m. to 3:00 p.m.

- At Group Health Corporation, a 650-employee health care facility center in Seattle, Washington, the entire staff of the radiology department with the exception of the office manager work compressed workweek schedules. Instituted as a way to extend services to patients, it has provided the added benefit of reducing burnout among the physicians.

- In Maricopa County, Arizona, concern over increasing traffic congestion and air pollution prompted officials to institute compressed workweeks. Approximately 60 percent of the 14,000 county employees are making use of this option.

Finding Flexibility on a Full-Time Schedule

Traffic tie-ups and a dreary commute of more than 20 hours a week sparked Pat Jackson's interest in changing her work schedule. "After our office moved to the suburbs, the thought of commuting more than 4 hours a day was shocking. For the first time I weighed the benefits of staying in my job or looking for something new closer to home."

A senior executive for a national disability organization in Bethesda, Maryland, Pat decided she wasn't ready to leave her job yet. She explains, "At the time there was great momentum building in the disability community in anticipation of the Americans with Disabilities Act (ADA). I wanted to be part of the programs I'd invested so much time and energy in developing."

Once Pat made up her mind to stay with the organization, she searched for a practical solution. With a high priority on keeping her salary and benefits in place, she looked into full-time options first. Committed to juggling a thirty-five-hour week during which she manages a staff of seven people with easing her commute, Pat found a happy medium in the compressed workweek arrangement.

Since working a similar schedule to her staff was high on her list, Pat cut her lunch hour in half and extended her workday by 1½ hours Monday through Thursday. By working four longer days, she cut out commuting on Fridays—a notorious day for Washington, D.C., traffic—and shortened her evening commute since a later departure time put her in traffic just past the peak of rush hour.

Pat has found the balance she was looking for in a compressed workweek schedule. Eager to share her success with others, she offers the following advice: "Good planning is essential to making a shortened workweek a success. I organize my schedule carefully to avoid taking work home with me and to accommodate the meetings I must attend. When I have to work or travel out-of-town on a Friday,

(continued on next page)

> *(continued from previous page)*
> I earn comp time and, if a pressing matter spills over to Friday, my staff knows they can reach me at home."
>
> Pat also acknowledges that the age of her children has been an advantage. Since her boys are in their teens and no longer need day care before and after school, she has the flexibility to switch her day off when the need arises.

THE FLEXTIME OPTION

Flextime is a full-time schedule that gives you the freedom to start and leave work at times that are most convenient to you. The flexible period is generally at the beginning and the end of each day with a core period when all employees must be present. While a flextime schedule can be used on an individual basis, it is usually implemented on a department- or company-wide basis with the employer determining the range of "flexing."

First used in Germany in the 1960s to alleviate traffic problems, flextime was introduced in the United States by Hewlett-Packard in 1972 as a low-cost benefit to employees at its plant in Waltham, Massachusetts. In the last twenty years, flextime has evolved to answer the needs of an increasingly diverse work force. It can be found in nearly every industry and is the most prevalent work schedule variation used by federal and state government agencies.

Effect on Pay and Benefits

Flextime has no effect on either your pay or benefits package because you're still working the same amount of time each week.

Schedule Variations

Core time and the flexband are the two main components of a flextime policy. Core time—the hours during which all employees must be on the job—is the time of day when most business is conducted. The flexband is the time during which employees may vary arrival and departure times.

Flextime arrangements encompass a variety of schemes. The most common arrangement provides for a morning flexband from 7:00 a.m. to 10:00 a.m. and an afternoon flexband from 3:30 p.m. to 6:30 p.m., with the core time in the middle of the day (10 a.m. to 2:00 p.m.). One person may choose to start work at 8:00 a.m. and end at 4:30 p.m., while another person in the same department might start at 7:30 a.m. and end at 4:00 p.m.

A midday flex period lets employees take 2 hours off around lunch time in exchange for working the same number of hours at the beginning or end of the day. It is popular with working parents and others with midday obligations. Here are some typical flextime schedules.

Without a midday flex period:

Flex start time	Core time	Flex quit time
7:30 a.m.–10 a.m.	10 a.m.–2 p.m.	2 p.m.–5:30 p.m.

With a midday flex period:

Flex start time	Core time	Midday flextime	Core time	Flex quit time
7 a.m.–9 a.m.	9 a.m.–12 noon	12 noon–2 p.m.	2 p.m.–4 p.m.	3 p.m.–6 p.m.

Other terms used by organizations to describe various types of "flexes" are gliding time, variable day, maxiflex, staggered hours, and "mother's hours."

Advantages and Disadvantages

Flextime offers an attractive option to the rigid 8-hour workday. Here are some reasons:

- There is little, if any, adjustment to your work load.
- You get a flexible schedule without reducing your pay and benefits.
- Your commuting time may be shortened if you travel during off-peak hours.
- You can tailor your work schedule to your children's school schedule.
- It gives you more time with family members in the morning or evening.
- You're more productive because you can work during your peak periods.

The drawbacks to flextime are few but should not be overlooked:

- If you start your workday earlier than most of your colleagues, you may find it hard to leave while others are still working.
- If your job requires constant interaction with other employees or clients, it may be harder to adopt a flextime schedule.

What Employers Think

Employers generally perceive flextime as a low-cost employee benefit that enhances morale and reduces or eliminates tardiness. Well-defined parameters and the potential to improve office coverage and extend hours of service have cleared the way for its acceptance among many private and public employers.

When one employee works a flextime schedule, it is relatively straightforward to deal with. However, when several employees or an entire department is involved, ensuring that all staffing and work-flow requirements are met can be difficult at times.

Flextime is the most prevalent work schedule variation in state governments. All fifty states, including the District of Columbia, have had some type of flextime policy in place for five years or longer.

Flextime is also widely used in the private sector. A case in point is the Transamerica Occidental Life Insurance Company in Los Angeles, which reduced employee turnover by 45 percent when it made flextime available to its workers. An overwhelming 90 percent of the employees use this option, mostly to take care of early morning and late afternoon child-care arrangements.

Planning for Flexibility

Aiming to stretch limited resources further and extend services to students during evening hours, Sue Pervi, vice-president of administration at the Catholic University of America, introduced flexible schedules in departments throughout the university. No stranger to the benefits of flextime, Sue turned to this option herself when

(continued on next page)

(continued from previous page)

her daughter's skating career escalated and demanded more of her time during the week.

Sue's challenge was squeezing in a 180-mile round-trip drive to Delaware every Tuesday afternoon so her daughter could train with a private coach. Sue felt she could fit the drive into her schedule by juggling her hours and taking some work on the road with her. She explains, "By making minor adjustments to my work schedule and planning my calendar six months out, I felt I could handle the drive once a week. The biggest challenge has been planning back-up arrangements on short notice when a crisis at work prevents me from getting away from the office on time."

Sue's first move was to get her staff on board. Not wanting the department heads who report to her to feel shortchanged, she rearranged her weekly meetings with them to avoid Tuesdays, a day she usually felt rushed. She also got her secretary used to putting aside "portable" work, such as reading and answering correspondence, for Sue to take with her on the road. Her cellular phone and laptop computer also figured prominently into her plan. "I keep in touch with the office by car phone when I'm on the road and have arranged a quiet place to work while I'm at the rink," Sue said. "I'm very productive during those 3 hours and accomplish things I don't have time for at the office."

Sue's search for ways to be more efficient has spilled over into her daily hour-long commute to and from the office. "I've started requesting the professional journals I subscribe to on tape," she says. "They make the ride go a little faster and I get my required 'reading' done before I even get to work."

Sue's story makes the point well that keeping an open mind about how and where work can be accomplished is a key to the success of a flextime schedule. Communicating her needs to her staff, rearranging meetings, and making the most of available technology allows Sue to carry on business as usual—just in a slightly different way.

THE TELECOMMUTING OPTION

Also known as flexiplace, work-at-home, and teleworking, the term telecommuting was coined by Los Angeles management consultant Jack Nilles twenty years ago, but it's only in the last five years that it has gained widespread appeal. Telecommuting—by whatever name you call it—is a work arrangement that gives employees the option to work a portion of their scheduled work hours off-site. Usually this has meant working at home, but it can also mean working at a branch office or other satellite facility.

In its early years telecommuting was done mostly by data-entry clerks, programmers, financial analysts, technical writers, and researchers. Today working off-site has expanded greatly; an estimated 6.6 million Americans are telecommuters, according to Link Resources, a New York consulting firm.[5] Many are professionals in fields such as marketing, law, and engineering who are taking advantage of the flexibility it offers.

Technological advances and a growing concern for the quality of our environment have pushed telecommuting ahead of the other options. Faxes, modems, and computers make it possible to work almost anywhere, at any time. And the Clean Air Act, passed in 1992 by Congress, has put added pressure on employers to find solutions in the workplace to reduce auto pollution from commuters.

Effect on Pay and Benefits

If you're working full-time, you'll continue to receive the same pay and benefits you'd receive if working on-site full-time. However, if you're combining this option with a reduced workweek, your pay and benefits will be determined by your company's policy on part-time employment.

Schedule Variations

Schedules for telecommuters vary widely. Telecommuters can work full-time or part-time. The amount of time spent working in the office versus off-site depends on the nature of the job and individual circumstances. Most telecommuters, however, spend at least half of their time in the office.

A New Road to Work
&.

A government experiment with telecommuting is reducing Judy Shifflett's stress level as well as her 4-hour commute from a rural town in Virginia to the Pentagon; now she only makes that trip three days a week. That's because Judy is able to take advantage of one of the first satellite "telework" centers to open in the United States.

Judy, a program analyst for the Department of the Army, works two days a week at one of four family-friendly work centers being set up in the Washington, D.C. area. Long commutes are the norm there for many government workers. Judy and her boss had considered a work-at-home arrangement, but the idea got derailed when the logistics of setting up a compatible computer system in Judy's home got too complicated and expensive. When she read about the government's pilot program at the Shenandoah Valley Telecommuting Center 25 minutes from home, she jumped at the chance to sign up.

Judy requested information on the program from the General Services Administration (GSA), the agency responsible for funding and launching the centers. Armed with the details, she went to her supervisor with a new plan for coping with her commute. Judy recalls, "I didn't have much selling to do to my supervisor at all."

Aware of Judy's long commute and the possibility of losing her to a job closer to home, Judy's supervisor welcomed the idea. She says, "Judy is a wonderful employee I certainly don't want to lose. An opportunity for her to telecommute seemed like a perfect solution for both of us."

The guidelines for the pilot program are simple. Having earned a "fully successful" rating or better on past performance reviews, Judy easily passed the first hurdle of eligibility. Since most of her time is spent on the phone or at the computer running statistics or answering correspondence, Judy's job is a good match for telecommuting. The

(continued on next page)

(continued from previous page)

fact that her job requires little "face time" with her supervisor, co-workers, or the public was also a selling point.

Modeled after telecommuting programs at large corporations, Judy and her boss had to sign a Telecommuter's Work Agreement, which outlined the terms of the one-year pilot program and the specifics, such as the hours and days Judy would work at the satellite office. They initially discussed her using the center three days a week but settled on two so that other people in the division could get used to the idea. Judy says, "There's one manager I work for who frequently needs graphs and charts on short notice. To help him contend with the days I'm off-site, we thought it would be better if I worked at the center just a couple of days a week."

In ideal telecommuting arrangements, the telecommuter and supervisor have a relationship built on trust. And this is true of Judy and her boss, too. "I know what I'm supposed to do and I get it done," Judy says. "A lot of my work is judged on volume. My supervisor can see for herself how much I've gotten done at the center when I have a stack of correspondence for her to sign." She adds, "I know I wouldn't be here if there was any doubt about my work."

Her supervisor agrees. "Not every employee is suited to telecommuting. They must be personally responsible, self-motivated, and technically capable of working without supervision," she says. "I know Judy will do her work whether she's here or she's there. She doesn't need me watching over her."

Like most telecommuters, Judy found she was more productive away from the interruptions at the office. But she wasn't expecting the personal benefits that have come her way. No longer captive to a 9:00 p.m. bedtime to rise by 3:30 a.m. two days a week, Judy attended her first PTA meeting in six years. She's also found that working nearby part of the time has helped ease the stress that her full-time career and long commute puts on her family.

In the past she thought about leaving her job in Washington and

(continued on next page)

(continued from previous page)

finding something closer to home, but she would have had to give up a lot. A twenty-six-year veteran of the government, Judy explains, "My family is so important, but on the other hand I have to think down the road to retirement. I just have too much to lose by starting over again with a new employer close to home."

Advantages and Disadvantages

For many, telecommuting is an attractive option for the following reasons:

- It usually reduces your commuting time.
- It often lets you work in a more relaxed work environment.
- You can be more productive because you can use part of your commuting time to work, you're away from distractions at the office, and you can adjust your schedule to fit your "internal clock."
- This option gives you the freedom to work independently and at your own pace.
- It opens up job opportunities to people in rural areas and those unable to travel long distances to work.
- It adds to your income by reducing transportation, clothing, and lunch expenses.

The drawbacks to telecommuting include:

- You may be unavailable for impromptu meetings.
- You may feel isolated; you may be left out of the decision-making loop.
- It requires self-discipline to work on your own.
- It may create a potential obstacle to career mobility.

What Employers Think

Perhaps more than any other option, employers see telecommuting as a mutual benefit to themselves and to their employees. Some employers have adopted telecommuting options because of a specific work-related problem, such as the need to reduce traffic congestion caused by the 1994 Los

Angeles earthquake. Others see it as a reasonable response to employee requests for different schedules to accommodate personal work styles, alleviate commuting problems, or to better manage family responsibilities.

Whatever the reason, telecommuting programs are springing up in both the public and private arenas. In the private sector, Bell Atlantic, Pacific Bell, U S WEST, and JC Penney instituted telecommuting on a company-wide basis following successful pilot programs.

In the public sector, the federal government took the lead when it introduced the Flexible Workplace Project on a pilot basis in 1990. A government-wide project, it opened up new opportunities for federal employees to work at home or at other approved sites away from the office for all or part of the workweek. In 1993, Congress, encouraged by national studies that showed telecommuting reduces traffic congestion, pollution, gasoline consumption, and accidents, took a giant step forward when it appropriated $5 million in seed money to establish family-friendly work centers in Virginia and Maryland for federal employees who have long commutes between their homes and Washington, D.C.

One concern shared by private and public sector employers is the cost effectiveness of telecommuting. Footing the bill for an employee to have an office at work and another one off site may be possible for a few employees but could be prohibitive on a larger scale. Warren Master, director of the General Services Administration's new telecommuting work center program, told the *Washington Post*: "The logistics and technology is fairly simple. The biggest question is how do you make this cost-effective so you're not paying double for the work space."[6] While the question of cost effectiveness lingers, the interest in telecommuting is skyrocketing. National estimates show that as many as 15 million people are expected to be telecommuting within the next ten years.[7]

OTHER FLEXIBLE WORK

ARRANGEMENTS

Here are some other, less common work arrangements you may encounter:

Phased retirement belongs to the family of part-time options. It allows workers who are nearing retirement to gradually reduce their work schedules over a period of time, generally six months to two years. An appealing option in the 70s and 80s, it has become less attractive during the past few years when most people were trying to hold on to their jobs, not retire early.

V-Time (voluntary reduced work time) is a voluntary time/income trade-off in which employees cut back their work hours and accept a corresponding reduction in pay. Often initiated by the employer as a cost-saving measure, it is usually used for a short period of time and guarantees employees a return to full-time status.

Work sharing is an involuntary arrangement used by employers during a recession or slow period in lieu of widespread layoffs. Work sharing does not mean that two workers share a specific job; rather it is a program in which all employees of the organization reduce their work hours and pay, take a corresponding reduction in pay, and in some instances receive partial unemployment payments.

Slot pooling provides employers with a mechanism to increase part-time jobs without reducing the number of budgeted full-time positions. For example, five attorneys might share three full-time slots and work a combined total of 15 days per week. Salaries are prorated according to the number of days each attorney works.

Extended workweek involves extending a 40-hour workweek over more than five days.

Compflex, a combination of a compressed workweek and a flextime schedule, is one example of how flexible work options are used together.

Leaves of absence are typically included in any discussion of flexible work arrangements. They are authorized periods of time away from work without the loss of employment rights. The leaves may be paid or unpaid and are usually extended for reasons such as family responsibilities, education, health care, or personal time.

TO SUM IT UP

✔ If you need the salary and benefits of a full-time job, consider compressed workweek, flextime, or full-time telecommuting.

✔ If you need more time for family, yourself, or personal interests, and can reduce your income and benefits, consider permanent part-time, job sharing, or part-time telecommuting.

✔ If you need the salary and benefits of a full-time job but want to reduce commuting time, consider compressed workweek or telecommuting.

✔ If you can reduce your income and benefits but want to retain status and responsibilities of your current job, consider job sharing. Permanent part-time can work, too, if your job is restructured properly.

✔ If you want to work from home, full- or part-time telecommuting is a good bet.

PART 2

Making Choices

CHAPTER 3

FITTING FLEXIBILITY INTO YOUR CAREER

Think of

your career as

the synergistic

combination of

your skills,

values, lifestyle,

and interests.

— *Jo-Ann Vega*

"I've found the best of both worlds." That's how so many people have described their new flexible jobs to us. And it's no wonder. You'll also feel personal satisfaction and emotional freedom when you find the right formula for mixing personal and professional goals.

The challenge of fitting flexibility into your career starts with making choices. You'll see for yourself that the answer lies entirely with you. How you perceive your own professional course, how well you are able to set realistic expectations, and the level of comfort you have with the choices you make along the way are at the heart of making a successful transition to a flexible job.

Trade-offs are a constant companion to flexibility—especially when you work part-time. Clearly, if you stick with a full-time option, you'll have fewer compromises to make regarding your career. The one exception may be telecommuting—if you end up working away from the office more than two days a week. Like a part-time schedule, it takes you out of the eye of your supervisor, and, for some managers, this lack of visibility sends a signal that your commitment is less than those who are constantly present. We've heard of cases where this attitude has slowed down career advancement. If you won't be spending as much time at your desk as you have in the past, look for our suggestions later in this chapter for ways to stay visible on the job.

As you consider flexibility and weigh the impact it might have on your career, there's one important thought to keep in mind: Career planning is a dynamic process. A choice you make today about the way you work probably won't last forever. Chances are, your personal circumstances and needs will change, and you may feel differently about work over time, too. Once you see your career as an evolving, ongoing process, you'll have an easier time of accepting how one decision fits into the many career decisions you'll make in the long run.

In this chapter we'll take a look at ways people are fitting flexibility into their careers and into their long-term career goals. Some have temporarily shelved the fast track to work part-time or even taken a step back in exchange for flexibility. Others have found the best solution is working for themselves, while still others have used creative strategies for keeping their careers moving forward as they cut back the number of hours they work.

As you read, keep in mind the differences between each of these work situations. What makes an excellent alternative solution in one job might not be feasible in another. And what works for someone else may not be the right choice for you. However, we think you'll see from the experiences of the people here that a little imagination and dedication to one's own priorities can make any career path possible.

CAREERS IN THE 90s

When you were a teenager or perhaps a college student, you probably never dreamed of some of the new career paths open to you today. Most of us grew up thinking that one day we'd enter the work force just as our fathers (and some of our mothers) before us did, making a long-term commitment to one field—and probably to one employer—and reaping the rewards of steady advancement, growing responsibilities, and regular salary increases.

But a changing economic and social picture has forced a new definition of career track on us. With the elimination of millions of middle management jobs over the past decade through downsizing in nearly every industry, we see our chances for the traditional career path dwindling. And the promotions and salary increases that we could once count on to fuel our enthusiasm are slower to come, as cost-conscious employers strive to do more with less.

The tumult of the 90s has left no one untouched. It's not at all uncommon for people from CEOs, custodians, and levels in between to job-hop from one employer to another as they become unwitting victims of corporate mergers, acquisitions, and downsizings. Dr. Ronald Krannich sums it up in his book *Careering and Re-careering for the 1990s*. He writes, "the 'one job, one career, one work life' phenomenon has all but ended for many occupations. The fifteen jobs, five careers, ten geographic moves, and many work lives phenomenon is now upon us."[1]

Clearly, corporate America is changing, and its work force is changing too. A ground swell of family values along with a greater emphasis on personal satisfaction has compelled people to search for new ways to be successful on their own terms. In fact, recent polls confirm we're reassessing our ideas toward work and career achievement.

Of the 1,000 people surveyed in a 1989 Robert Half International study, 82 percent of the women and 78 percent of the men said that they would choose a slower career path over faster career advancement in exchange for flexible full-time hours and more time with their families.[2] In a 1990 survey by the Roper Organization, 41 percent of the respondents said that leisure time came ahead of work as the "most important thing," compared to 36 percent who rated work above leisure. Just five years earlier, 46 percent of those surveyed had stated that work was most important, compared to only 33 percent who chose leisure.[3]

Some people searching for a better work/life balance are making more time for their personal lives by moving work down a notch on their list of priorities—and they don't regret it. Amy Saltzman, author of the book *Downshifting*, reports, "While the fast track and its accompanying imagery of career achievement still has its appeal, there is a pervasive feeling that we have drastically overemphasized its importance; that as individuals and as a society we need to reinvent our notion of success."[4]

Getting Off the Fast Track
?

Redefining success is often the first step in fitting flexibility into your career. For Tracy Keeter that meant jumping off the fast track. Reforming a workaholic life-style was her highest priority when she voluntarily left a full-time management job in which she was supervising a staff of sixteen people to take a part-time software position in another division of the company. She had enough of 60-, 70-, and in some cases, even 80-hour weeks. And she disliked

(continued on next page)

(continued from previous page)

being connected to a beeper 24 hours a day while managing the home front as a single parent. "I had been going too far, too fast, and I was just burned out," she told her shocked colleagues when she announced her intentions to scale back.

After she worked part-time for six months, the company asked Tracy to reorganize the work flow of four groups without restoring her supervisory responsibilities. Tracy countered with an offer to accept the responsibility, but only on a part-time basis, three days a week. They settled on four days a week. But after a corporate reorganization some eight months later, management again delivered a full-time ultimatum.

This time Tracy had to relent. The alternative of being laid off was one she couldn't afford. Tracy held fast to her goals of greater flexibility, however, and, when another corporate reorganization left her with a new supervisor, she again successfully negotiated a part-time position. For three years she worked part-time, earning outstanding reviews. Yet despite her excellent performance, whenever the subject of becoming a manager came up, she continued to run into resistance from senior management, who would not let part-time employees become managers.

"The answer for me was to get out," Tracy recalls. "I had to switch gears and move on to something else." After considering all her options, she left the company and started a home-based consulting business. Now she also sets her own rules and manages a schedule that allows her to spend guilt-free time with her children.

There's a lesson in Tracy's story. She had to make hard choices to keep her priorities intact, to keep her career moving without giving up the flexible schedule she felt was so important to her. In the end she made it work: she chose a series of tactics, culminating in a career shift into consulting.

CREATING NEW FEMALE ROLE MODELS

Since it became a household item in the 50s, television has provided a mirror image of the role women play in everyday life. Through the years we made coffee with the perfect wife and mother, June Cleaver; learned about working in a man's world from Mary Tyler Moore; and laughed with TV anchor cum Supermom Murphy Brown. But our latest role models are the real women we see on the screen every day. Television journalists like Jane Pauley and Katie Couric and public figures like First Lady Hillary Rodham Clinton and Supreme Court Justice Sandra Day O'Connor have talked openly about mixing motherhood with career.

Starting with June Cleaver, these women have chronicled the dramatic changes in women's roles over the last several decades. Most of us remember our mothers and our friends' mothers as homemakers. They were there when we set off in the morning and were waiting for us when we returned in the afternoon. If they longed to be out in the world of work, they seldom let on. The women we knew who worked full-time did so out of economic necessity or were single or childless. In those days women had two choices—become a career woman or a housewife. It was an either/or decision; few dared to mix the two.

The 70s and 80s brought major changes. Women entered a new era as they became better educated and moved up in male-dominated fields such as law, engineering, medicine, and business. They became successful attorneys, engineers, doctors, dentists, CPAs, and business leaders. Out of this new-found success in the workplace came a period of questioning in which women struggled to redefine their roles as professionals and as mothers. Some wanted to forge ahead on a career path to the top, delaying marriage and children until they felt well established in their careers. Others wrestled with wanting both family and career.

This pull of conscience and tradition on the one hand and new professional opportunities on the other gave us the Supermom—the woman who wanted to have it all, family and career, and all at once. However, it wasn't long before the stress of juggling a full-time career and family took its toll on these Supermoms. Within a few short years the slogan became "Have it all, but not all at once." Unwilling to be bound by the limitations of choosing between family and career, women sounded the call for flexible work arrangements and family-friendly programs.

In their efforts to balance career and family, many of the women we interviewed felt they were navigating uncharted waters, unsure of what they might find along the way. They found few who could offer advice because no one had been there yet. MaryAnn Simon, a trial lawyer married to another attorney, articulated the dilemma so many women who are part of dual-career families feel: "There are no role models to show us what to do when both of us have to be in court and our two-year-old comes down with chickenpox."

For their book, *Answers to the Mommy Track*, Trudi Ferguson and Joan Dunphy surveyed thirty-five women who had reached the top of their professions to find out how they balanced motherhood with their professional lives. In response to a question on role models, 43 percent of them stated that they had no role models and another 31 percent cited their mothers as being their main source of inspiration.[5] And for the most part these role-model mothers did not work out of the house.

Working women today must create their own role models by drawing on the experiences of several people, like their mothers and fathers and public figures, to find ways to combine career aspirations with the joys of raising a family. To this they've added their own set of values and expectations, creating a new set of role models for those who follow.

Many women traveling in these new directions are using flexible work arrangements to ease the way. Some are scaling back temporarily, while others are striking out on their own. Still others are shifting the focus of their careers or changing careers altogether.

And for many, choosing flexibility means coming to terms with the trade-offs. Deborah Swiss and Judith Walker write about it in their book, *Women and the Work/Family Dilemma*. Of the 902 Harvard business, law, and medical school graduates they surveyed, 766 of them believe that reducing hours of work is detrimental to a woman's career. Nevertheless, 70 percent of the women with children decreased their hours after the birth of their first child. "Knowing that the traditional rules of a male-dominated work culture challenge their role as a parent, the Harvard women demonstrated a fierce determination to forge new definitions for being an involved parent and a committed professional," Swiss and Walker write.[6]

The underlying message is that women are taking control of their personal and professional lives and choosing what's best for them during different times of their lives. By breaking with the past and establishing new patterns, they're setting the stage for the next generation.

The New "Career-Speak"

People who plan their careers around flexibility are often committed to change. Here are some of the terms we hear today that describe this new breed of worker:

- *Downshifters* jump off the fast track to reduce stress and strike a balance between work and personal interests.
- *Re-careerers* repeatedly update and acquire new skills to stay marketable and to give themselves the flexibility to change careers if they want to or are forced to.
- *Plateauers* intentionally put their careers on hold by turning down promotions in favor of devoting time and energy to other activities.
- *Portfolio people* develop an array or portfolio of skills that allows them to move easily among a variety of assignments or jobs.
- *Casserole careerers* juggle many jobs at once in lieu of one full-time job, either to make ends meet or to build new skills for a subsequent career.
- *Career shifters, career changers, or career switchers* reduce stress or replace a lost job by applying their skills and experience to a new job in a related field or the to same job in a less stressful field.

WHAT'S NEXT FOR MEN?

Old habits die hard, as the saying goes, especially when it comes to changing the way men think about work. Understandably they're way behind the curve on flexibility. For the most part, men still see flexibility as a women's issue. The few exceptions are working fathers, but even they are not in a big rush to jump on the bandwagon.

This is evidenced in a study of the nation's largest 1,000 companies, conducted by Robert Half International in 1990. The survey found that while 31 percent of the companies offered some form of paternity leave, only about 1 percent of eligible employees took advantage of it.[7] And surveys conducted at Du Pont and Levi Strauss, two companies that offer generous family leave benefits to men and women, came to virtually the same conclusion.[8]

Men have several strikes against them when it comes to taking family leave and using flexible schedules. The fact that the average working woman still makes less than her male counterpart means most families can't make do if the father works part-time or chooses to take an unpaid paternity leave. The utter lack of male role models working in nontraditional ways in upper management is a great deterrent. And the fear of running into their own version of the glass ceiling—an invisible barrier to promotion that many women in particular must struggle against (see "Overcoming Barriers," later in this chapter)—has also had a chilling effect on men who are thinking about taking advantage of flexible work policies.

In a *Washington Post* article, Marcia Brumit Kropf, a research group leader at Catalyst, a national research and advisory organization in New York, hit the nail on the head. She said, "Making family leave available isn't enough; companies have to encourage men to take advantage of the programs." [9] Indeed, several men we spoke with voiced their concern about subtle and not so subtle discrimination in the workplace. Roger Milton is one of them. An associate on the fast track at a law firm in Chicago, Roger talked to the managing partner about working part-time for six months following the birth of his twin sons. He was told, "The policies are there for you to do it, but I wouldn't advise it." Concerned about his chances for partnership, Roger backed off and hired a full-time nanny instead.

While women have one foot planted firmly at work and the other one solidly rooted at home, men are almost entirely grounded at work. Joseph H. Pleck, a research associate at Wellesley College's Center for Research on Women, said, "The attitude is actually out there that yes, fathers should be involved." But that conflicts with another prevailing attitude: "that fathers should not reduce their commitment to the job and never forget that their primary responsibility is to earn an income."[10]

One new father, who chose to work part-time for three years until his daughter entered preschool, explains the mixed feelings men have this way: "A lot of men have biases within themselves. We all grew up with the stereotype that it's the man's job to bring home the money. It's a real cultural thing that men feel guilty if they're not working and women feel guilty if they're not staying at home."[11]

The prognosis for men who want flexibility on the job is encouraging, but they clearly have lots of catching up to do.

THE PART-TIME FACTOR

What can happen to your career when you decide to work part-time? Ideally, nothing should, but in reality we know that's not the case. Of all the alternative work arrangements, the one likely to have the greatest impact on your career path is part-time work. Why is this so? There's no single, simple reason. A combination of factors at your workplace mixed with your own expectations will ultimately affect your career advancement path.

To start with, look at where you are in your career. Other factors figure in, too: The number of hours you work in relation to your colleagues, the type of work you do, and the practices and policies of your employer all play a role.

When professionals work part-time, they find themselves in the precarious position of setting limits in a culture that thrives on total commitment. This culture values work above personal concerns, often measures devotion in terms of "face time" spent in the office and asks for total availability to clients and management. By breaking with these conventions and placing limits on the extent of one's work life, part-timers are often put in the position of trading career advancement for flexibility.

Not everyone who pursues a part-time schedule loses ground professionally, but more often than not they are seen as putting their careers on hold. Mary Rehm, a supervising legal secretary at a law firm in Seattle, Washington, was told "you can't be a supervisor anymore," when she approached the firm's administrator about working part-time. Interested in working fewer hours and in a less stressful job, Mary explains that, "at that point I was willing to give up a career step for family and peace of mind."

Scaling back to part-time poses no problem for some of the people we've interviewed. Like Mary, they're satisfied with the job they have and content to stay where they are.

Others we've talked to struggle with the psychological gremlins of guilt and what they perceive to be stagnation in their careers. For Jane Lyder, an attorney in the Office of the Legislative Counsel at the U.S. Department of Interior, there's a definite downside to working part-time. "There are limits to what you can do and in your promotion potential," she contends. "I would never have been in this job this long without moving up if I weren't working part-time. I don't really see any opportunities for me on the management level if I keep my flexible schedule. So for me it's constantly debating whether to work full-time or not. I feel if I want to move ahead I have to work full-time."

Overcoming Barriers

If working part-time means giving up supervisory or managerial responsibilities, you may find, like Jane and like Tracy Keeter earlier in this chapter, that compromises are hard to accept. But encountering barriers is nothing new for professional women. A case in point is the notorious glass ceiling, which, as much as we might hate to admit it, is alive and well in the 1990s. The term "glass ceiling," coined in 1987, refers to an invisible barrier preventing entrance to the top jobs. Swiss and Walker write about this phenomenon in their book. "The glass ceiling has remarkably few cracks," they contend, "despite the number of talented women who have entered the traditional male-dominated professions of business, law, and medicine."[12]

And, they believe, things can get even harder when working women become mothers and try to maintain the same career momentum as their male colleagues. An additional barrier, the maternal wall, as Swiss and Walker refer to it, prevents these women from even reaching the glass ceiling above them. Women who must work around family obligations are often seen as unprofessional, uncommitted, and lacking the "necessities" to manage. The maternal wall shows up in the form of missed promotions and assignments. These are the same barriers women often run into when choosing flexibility over a rigid, traditional work schedule.

Taking Advantage of Career Opportunities

Fortunately for some people, working a flexible schedule doesn't always mean putting a career on hold or taking a step backwards. It can mean promotions and career advancement, as it did for Cynthia Ford, a public relations specialist in the insurance industry, who was promoted to a more senior position even though she works just three days a week. And as it did for Jenny Rieves, who moved from a sales position to an account executive position while working four days a week for a large computer company.

In some cases, moving into a flexible arrangement may actually enhance your career. A good example is Laura Embrey, a senior analyst in the advertising and sales promotion department at USAir's headquarters in Arlington, Virginia. When she decided to scale back her full-time hours after the birth of her child, she was an analyst in the pricing department. If she had chosen to stay where she was, her only option to work part-time would have meant transferring to the ticket counter at the airport—a definite regression in her career. "Returning to the field would have meant taking a step backward. I would have been out of the loop for a couple of years and might have had difficulty getting back at all," she says.

Instead, a chance encounter with a colleague in the company parking lot opened up a new and challenging opportunity for Laura. Jean Buckley, a senior analyst, was looking for a job-share partner. Laura was able to apply for the job under a recently implemented job-share program at USAir. "To be able to go into a new department at a senior analyst level and get the opportunity to learn new things has been great for my career," she says. "But it was a risk. I was put back on a probationary period and faced being out of a job altogether if it hadn't worked out."

Karen Roesler is another job sharer who parlayed her job into a promotion when she moved up from the assistant director position at the Wallingford Public Library in Wallingford, Connecticut, to share the director's position with Leslie Scherer.

While Laura and Karen were both in the right place at the right time, their situations are not uncommon. They both seized an opportunity and saw the possibilities in trying something new.

Part-Time Work as a Career Strategy

Becky Kline went from full-time work to a part-time consulting job after the birth of her first son. That was six years ago. Since then she has positioned herself on a well-defined career path that still allows her to have time with her children. "When I started a family, I didn't assume I couldn't work anymore," says Becky, who now works from her home as human resources director for a start-up company in Fairfax, Virginia. "To me it wasn't an all-or-nothing situation."

Becky is planning her career around part-time work, an innovative strategy that has given her the best of both worlds. "What I'm doing now," she explains, "is preparing myself for the future. I don't look at my experience in the short term. I look at it in terms of how it's going to help me in five or ten years when I may want to go back to work full-time."

While Becky has found this arrangement to be the best solution for her current needs, she acknowledges there have been compromises. She has to be more selective about the projects she accepts, sometimes turning down interesting work due to time limitations. While she commands a competitive salary, Becky has lost quite a bit in benefits. But the positives clearly far outweigh the negatives. "Working part-time allows me to continue pursuing a career on my own terms. I'd much rather keep my hand in my career now than start over again in five or ten years," she contends.

Planning Ahead for Part-Time

By planning ahead while she was still in graduate school, Tricia Pullen was able to preserve her career as a scientist when it came time to raise a family.

"I'm sad not to go to sea any longer," says Tricia, a research oceanographer with the National Oceanographic and Atmospheric Administration (NOAA) in Seattle. "I enjoyed that."

An expert in the use of acoustic Doppler technology, Tricia had gone to sea on thirty-day cruises for more than ten years in order to collect data for research projects that she proposed, won funding for, and managed. Anticipating marriage and children, Tricia had decided not to go on for her doctoral degree, feeling that it would be too hard later in her career to manage the transition in and out of Ph.D.-level work to accommodate the needs of a family. When a husband and children came along several years later than she expected, she decided that a scaled-back arrangement would be her best option.

"There are side effects," Tricia says. "I cannot do the same job part-time that I could do full-time." She gave up writing grant proposals, managing programs from beginning to end, and presenting papers at meetings. This allowed her to focus on her family life while she continued with her first love, research. She chose to work every Monday, Wednesday, and Thursday, eight hours a day, so that she'd never be away from the office more than one day at a time to establish a period of continuity in the week and feel like a true team member capable of fighting for the projects she cared about most.

On one particular project involving the Doppler, she feared she wouldn't get to work on the data collected because a full-time colleague received the assignment. But Tricia made herself available to research errors and solve problems as they arose. "I developed solutions and wrote papers on my findings," she says. "So now I've taken over working with the data, which is what I thought I wouldn't be able to do."

Keeping Visible in a Full-Time World

How do you let your employer know you're just as committed as the next person even though you're away from the office more than others? A work culture that measures devotion in terms of face time spent in the office puts an extra burden on part-timers. You can get around some of these traditional hang-ups and show you mean business by making sure you see yourself as you want to be seen by your colleagues. Then stop at nothing to keep your face and your name in the mix of your organization. Here are a few more suggestions for ways to show your commitment:

- Strive for high visibility with your employer and among your colleagues by lobbying for high-profile assignments that fit your skills and excite your professional senses.
- Be flexible so that you can meet your employer's needs. Anticipate management "crunch" times and make every effort to be responsive.
- Develop allies in the office. When your name comes up, make sure it's in a positive, can-do light.
- Emphasize your career aspirations. This will increase your credibility and keep your colleagues focused on your achievements and the quality of your work instead of on your family and personal matters.
- Keep your network intact. Don't let old contacts slip away. You never know when you'll be job hunting again or looking for clients to work with as a consultant.
- Stay active in your field by serving on the board of directors of a professional organization, incorporating your area of expertise whenever possible.
- Continue networking in a style that suits your schedule and budget. If you don't have the time or money to attend association conventions and meetings, keep in touch with your colleagues by phone. Send holiday greeting cards or mail FYI newspaper articles. Stop in occasionally for visits at their office.
- Always plan for your next career move. Build a file on employers you'd like to work for.

Staying Valuable to Your Company

Mary Ellen Austin knows what it means to stay visible and manage a part-time career. After five years of working part-time she was promoted to associate partner at Andersen Consulting. It took her three years longer than her peers, but "that was only fair," she says.

As only the second part-time manager to make it to associate partner, Mary Ellen knows how much you have to depend on a good support system, both at home and in the office. "The partner I work for is very supportive," Mary Ellen says. "He doesn't expect me to come in on my days off unless there is a pressing need. I also have a wonderful secretary who knows how to handle client calls."

Mary Ellen also attributes some of her success to her ability to say no. The nature of Mary Ellen's work allows her a certain degree of freedom in picking and choosing assignments. She successfully integrated her part-time schedule into those choices. She is fortunate to have the authority to delegate work, which in her position is key to ensuring proper coverage of her client accounts. "I probably think about delegating more than most people do when I'm setting up a job. I make sure I have someone who can handle himself or herself when I'm not there."

As an associate partner, Mary Ellen will continue working three days a week as she plans for another situation where flexibility will be vital: the birth of her third child. While there is no guarantee that she will advance to partner while still working part-time, she judges that sacrifice to be fair and one she's willing to make. "I feel like I gave up something from a career standpoint," she admits, "but I gained a lot by having the chance to spend more time with my kids. That, to me, is a great trade-off."

Mary Ellen's story points out perhaps the most critical aspect of seeking flexibility in your work situation: Keep your expectations realistic and then achieve everything you can within those tempered goals. Working part-time does not have to signal an end to the serious nature of your work. It simply requires adaptation.

YOUR OWN MEASURE OF SUCCESS

People seek flexibility for their own unique reasons. And, likewise, the definition of a successful arrangement is different for each person. For people working part-time, that success can bring with it trade-offs and compromises. However, you've seen how people like Becky Kline created a trade-off by using today's part-time activities as a springboard to possible full-time commitments later on. Others, like Mary Ellen Austin, compromised on career advancement in the short term in order to gain long-term career success.

For Tracy, Becky, Tricia, and Mary Ellen, success means something different. What all these women have in common is that they're all in successful work arrangements because they defined their priorities and goals early on and set everything into motion around them. You can do the same. Here are some pointers:

- **Set realistic expectations.** Trying to be all things to all people will eventually burn you out.
- **Redefine your image of success.** At one time it may have been a high salary or a senior position in the organization. Today it may be preserving your career while having enough time for yourself, your family, or other personal interests.
- **Get beyond the guilt.** If you work part-time, don't apologize for not being available 100 percent of the time at home or at the office. Your outlook will set the pace for how others accept you and the choices you've made.
- **Be prepared to make trade-offs, but also be sure the trade-offs are worth it to you.** Re-evaluate your career at least once a year to stay on track with short- and long-term goals.
- **Make the most of what you're doing.** Every job you succeed at adds something of value to your resume and builds on your career. If you feel your flexible schedule is holding you back in your current job, look for new opportunities that build on your strengths and skills.

TO SUM IT UP

✔ Career planning is a dynamic process.

✔ Be prepared to make changes along the way.

✔ Look for guidance and support from colleagues, friends, and family when making choices about your own career.

✔ Be prepared to make trade-offs if you work part-time.

✔ Be creative in thinking about how to keep your career moving forward.

✔ Find creative strategies to remain visible in the eyes of your employer.

✔ Set goals and define priorities when you're planning your career around flexibility.

CHAPTER 4

FITTING FLEXIBILITY INTO YOUR BUDGET

You can't

always get

what you want.

But if you try

sometimes . . .

you get what

you need.

— *Keith Richards
and Mick Jagger*

Most choices we face about life-style come down to a trade-off between time and money. If you're seeking more of one, there's a good chance you'll have to give up some of the other. Making choices and learning to live with compromises is a big part of fitting flexibility into your life. For some of us that's easier to do than for others. But once you've found the right mix of time and money, you'll probably agree that the trade-offs are worth it.

Note: If you're considering only full-time work options, skip ahead to chapter 5 since your salary and benefits won't be affected by any flexible full-time schedule you arrange.

The toughest choices often come with working part-time. Take Vicki Patterson, a school administrator and guardian of two teen-aged grandchildren. Vicki needed more time to supervise her grandchildren after school but couldn't sacrifice much of her income to do it. She said, "The insanity had to stop. My budget was tight, but something had to go if I was going to raise my grandchildren in a way I could be proud of."

As the sole breadwinner in her household, Vicki had to hang on to her health benefits, which meant working at least 35 hours a week. She restructured her schedule to start working at 7:30 a.m. instead of 8:30 a.m. and to leave every afternoon at 2:30 p.m. instead of 4:30 p.m. to reach home in time to beat the school bus. Vicki said, "I made the small sacrifice of starting the day earlier and the bigger sacrifice of a 12.5 percent pay cut, but in the long run it was worth it to have peace of mind."

Like many people who make a successful life-style change, once Vicki set priorities for the time and money she wanted, she was able to zero in on the schedule that would work the best and the salary and benefits she needed to make ends meet.

For Vicki, the solution was to work part-time. That may also be the answer for you. If not, don't give up—there are several other options for you to consider. In this chapter, we'll discuss the bottom line of choosing between a full- or part-time job. Quite simply, either you can afford to work part-time or you can't. And it all boils down to more than a part-time paycheck. Access to employee benefits—health insurance, a funded retirement plan, and paid leave days are money in the bank instead of money out of your pocket. Whether you're crafting a new salary and benefits plan for a full-time job you're redesigning to part-time or you're negotiating a part-time job with a new employer, you can't afford to overlook these valuable assets.

FLEXIBILITY AND MONEY

Money is important to all of us, but just how important is another question. Maybe it's a question you haven't asked yourself lately, but it's one you should answer when you're thinking about fitting flexibility into your budget. If your job pays for the roof over your head, puts food on the table, or provides you and your family with health insurance, the compromises of working part-time are likely to be far greater than if you bring home a second income that pays for the "extras"—a ski vacation in Vail or frequent dining out.

But simple math and the household budget don't necessarily add up to how you feel about making money. The amount of money we make also buys us status, recognition among our peers, independence, and a sense of security. Indeed, you may feel more conflicted about sacrificing these intangibles than you do about giving up a vacation or delaying the purchase of a new car. If you're having trouble deciding between making more money or having more time, consider easing into a part-time arrangement by gradually cutting your hours back or starting out with a three-month trial period to see if the trade-offs are a good fit for you.

Can You Afford to Cut Back?

Deanne Roads and her husband had always planned to move from their two-bedroom apartment into their own house before starting a family. But little David arrived before they had saved up enough for the down payment. Wanting more time with her new son, Deanne decided to cut back her full-time schedule, which meant putting a new house on hold.

Like Deanne, you may be convinced that working part-time is the answer, but look before you leap to be certain you can afford it. Take the time to figure out where your money is going each month. Add up your fixed expenses such as the mortgage or rent, car payment(s), commuting, food, and utilities. Then tally the "extras," which might include entertainment, vacations, eating out, and household help. Look for the places you can cut back in both areas to come up with a smaller livable budget.

If you want to work fewer days a week, you can get a pretty good idea of how much you can afford to cut back by doing some quick math. As a rule of thumb, you'll lose 20 percent of your salary for every full day you don't work. See how much income you'd be left with if you worked two, three, or four days a week. Compare that with the livable budget you totaled above to arrive at a starting point for trimming your schedule.

It wasn't until Carol Mulholland took this important first step that she could decide how many days a week to devote to her studies. She says, "I really wanted to work three days a week so I could get my master's degree. But when I figured out how much money I'd bring home, I decided I couldn't swing it." Carol settled on working three days a week for the fall semester and four days a week the rest of the year. "With a little creative budgeting and cutting back on the extras, I managed to stay on track with my degree and pay the bills on time," she says.

Even if you bring home a smaller paycheck, you may find some "hidden benefits" to cutting back your hours, especially when you work fewer days a week. Eating lunch out less frequently, buying fewer clothes for work, and reducing dependent care costs can give you more disposable income. And if you and your spouse file a joint tax return, you may find it easier to swallow the tax bill if your reduced income puts you in a lower tax bracket.

When it comes to the trade-offs between time and money, working mothers seem to feel the greatest pinch. Jill Kimble, a community relations representative who works part-time at a Fortune 500 company in Cleveland, told us, "By the time I get back and forth from work and pay the baby-sitter, I'm just breaking even."

If you find yourself in this dilemma, there are two ways to look at it. Either the professional and psychological rewards of working outweigh the monetary gains or it's not worth it to work unless you can add significantly to the family coffers. Obviously, there's no right or wrong answer because it's different for everyone. But remember, the decision to work part-time or to step out of the work force doesn't have to last forever.

FLEXIBILITY AND BENEFITS

Employee or "fringe" benefits are an important part of your total compensation package. They only enter the flexibility picture when you're looking for a part-time job or when you're thinking of redesigning the job you have from full- to part-time. Usually worth several thousand dollars—up to 41 percent of a full-timer's pay according to one 1991 U.S. Department of Labor study[1]—benefits are a precious commodity to part-timers who don't routinely receive them.

Before settling on a part-time arrangement, size up what your current or potential employer is willing to offer you in the way of a benefits package. If you find out you won't be paid for sick and vacation leave, and you don't have the safety net of health insurance from a spouse, the cost of working part-time may be out of your reach. But don't give up on finding flexibility. Numerous variations on telecommuting, flextime, and compressed work-week schedules offer good alternatives to full-time workers (see chapter 2).

Benefits in the Public Sector

If you work for the federal government and choose to scale back your hours, you're covered by the Federal Employees Part-Time Career Employment Act of 1978. The act guarantees you prorated benefits if you work 20 hours or more a week and you're at a GS-15 level or lower.

At the state level, there are widespread differences in the types of benefits offered to part-timers. Currently, Oregon is the only state providing full benefits to part-time workers, regardless of the number of hours worked. Fifteen other states prorate benefits for all part-timers no matter how many hours they work. And the remaining states use a variety of schemes for determining benefits. Massachusetts, for example, offers full health benefits and prorated vacation and sick leave to all part-time workers, whereas state employees in Louisiana must work 30 or more hours a week to receive prorated health benefits and 20 hours or more a week to get vacation and sick leave.

Benefits in the Private Sector

Employers in the private sector are all over the map when it comes to benefits for part-timers. You'll find everything from fully paid benefits to a prorated package to none at all. If your employer provides benefits to part-timers, the number of hours you work has direct bearing on the benefits you'll get. Here are just a few examples of what you can expect:

- Health and other insurances are available to you at no increased cost; your paid leaves and retirement plan are prorated.
- Health and other insurances are available to you but at a higher premium; your paid leave and retirement plan are prorated.
- Health and other insurances are unavailable to you, but you'll get a prorated retirement plan and prorated paid leaves.

Historically, part-timers have lagged behind full-timers when it comes to receiving equitable benefits packages. In December 1992, the U.S. Department of Labor confirmed this point when it released the results of its first comprehensive survey of companies with 100 or more employees, which covered 31 million full-time workers and 5 million part-timers. Not surprisingly, part-timers fared the best in getting paid vacation time and the worst in being eligible for health insurance.

What was surprising, however, was the limited use of flexible benefit plans on the part of employers. Also called cafeteria plans, these programs allow employees to pick and choose the benefits they need the most, with a prorated allowance for part-timers. Even though these plans offer the easiest way for employers to extend equitable benefits to everyone, they were only available to 10 percent of full-time employees and 2 percent of part-timers in the study. Used primarily by the largest employers in the study, small to mid-size companies maintain they don't have the staff to administer a plan with so many options nor employee groups large enough to qualify for various insurances at competitive rates.

How Do Benefits for Part-Timers Stack Up
with What Full-Timers Get?

Benefit	% of Part-Time* Workers Eligible	% of Full-Time Workers Eligible
Paid vacation time	55	96
Paid holidays	47	92
Paid sick leave	30	67
Paid jury duty	45	86
Paid maternity leave	1	2
Paid paternity leave	less than 0.5	1
Employee assistance programs	31	56
Flexible benefit plans	2	10
Employer-subsidized child care	5	8
Eldercare	4	9
Wellness programs	16	35
Medical insurance	28	83
Dental insurance	18	60
Life insurance	31	94
Retirement plans	40	78

*Employees are classified as part-time in accordance with practices of surveyed establishments.

Source: U.S. Bureau of Labor Statistics, *Employee Benefits in Medium and Large Private Establishments, 1991.*

WHAT YOU NEED TO KNOW

ABOUT BENEFITS

Whether you're starting out in search of a new job or reducing your hours, you need to know the basics of benefits. In short, here's how they work:

Statutory benefits—Social Security and Medicare, unemployment insurance, and worker's compensation—are the only benefits every employer is required to provide to all employees, regardless of their work schedules. Two other categories, typically referred to as supplemental and compensatory benefits, are offered at the discretion of the employer. Basic supplemental benefits include various insurances such as medical, dental, life, accident, short- and long-term disability, and retirement plans. Compensatory benefits give you paid time off for vacations, illnesses, and federal holidays.

Benefits Your Employer Must Provide

The following is an overview of the benefits your employer must give you.

Social Security and Medicare
These are required for every American worker under the Federal Insurance Contributions Act (FICA). If you're employed, both you and your employer make equal contributions of 7.65 percent. If you're self-employed, you are responsible for paying the full 15.3 percent contribution yourself.

Generally, part-time workers do not increase the cost of an employer's contribution. An exception occurs when two part-timers share a job and each earns a salary above the maximum taxable earnings (in 1993, $57,600). The employer then pays twice as much in taxes.

Unemployment Insurance
This insurance is a combined federal-state program. The U.S. Department of Labor administers the federal portion, and state employment commissions set their own benefit structure, eligibility requirements, and financing methods. An employer pays both federal and state taxes to finance unemployment compensation, with the rate of tax determined by the employer's use of the fund. Employers who make the fewest withdrawals from the system pay the lowest taxes.

Since employers are required to pay unemployment taxes for every worker, employers who hire two part-time workers instead of one full-time worker pay unemployment insurance taxes twice. However, in some states, part-timers who are laid off find themselves ineligible for unemployment compensation if they worked too few weeks a year or haven't reached a certain level of earnings.

Under the current system, most states that pay unemployment compensation to part-timers require that they look for and accept a full-time job, if offered. In an effort to counter this discrimination against part-timers, Representative Pat Schroeder (D-Colorado) has introduced a bill called the Part-Time and Temporary Workers Protection Act, which would require states to pay unemployment compensation benefits to part-time workers without requiring them to accept offers of full-time work.

Worker's Compensation
This state program is designed to make employers liable for workplace accidents. Regulations and benefits vary widely from state to state. Even though full- and part-time employees are covered on the same basis, premiums for part-time employees are automatically prorated.

Supplemental Benefits

Supplemental benefits are offered at the discretion of your employer. The most common include insurances, retirement plans, financial assistance programs, and information and referral services.

Health Insurance
Ask anyone you know what they consider to be their most important benefit, and chances are they'll answer "health insurance." Today, health insurance premiums are driving up the employer's cost per worker faster than any other benefit. As companies seek to contain these costs, many are dropping part-timers from their health plans or requiring both full- and part-time employees to pay a higher percentage of their premiums. Even in this case though, your employee contribution is almost always less than if you had to go out and purchase the same level of insurance on your own.

According to a 1991 Hewitt Associates survey, medical benefits, whether fully paid by the employer or on a cost-sharing basis with the employer, were offered to 76 percent of part-timers working 30 hours or more a week, 61 percent working 20 to 29 hours, and only 20 percent working less than 20 hours per week. In many cases, employers who don't extend insurances to part-timers cite high administrative costs of offering and administering such programs to employees with varying schedules. In other cases, the employer's insurance provider has limited the policy to full-timers (usually defined as those working 30 hours per week) only.[2]

Disability Insurance
Short- and long-term disability plans supplement the public programs under social security, worker's compensation, and state disability plans. Short-term disability is usually tied to sick-leave policies and long-term programs pick up when the short-term benefits expire. When extended to part-timers, disability insurance is commonly prorated.

Life Insurance
Life insurance programs take a variety of forms and are usually linked to an employee's annual salary. Part-timers' benefits are usually prorated.

Retirement Plans
Employers in the private sector are not legally required to provide their workers with a retirement plan. But if they do, the plan must conform to regulations spelled out in the Employee Retirement Income Security Act (ERISA). Passed in 1974, ERISA's eligibility rules protect part-timers who work for firms offering pension plans, preventing their exclusion from retirement programs. Under ERISA, coverage must be provided to all employees 21 years of age, with one year of service, who work 1,000 hours or more each year. The 1,000 hours of work may be completed in 20 hours per week, or over six months full-time.

Other Supplemental Benefits
For years, most benefits were limited to health, disability, and life insurance programs. Changes in the composition of the work force, specifically the increase of women in the workplace, has motivated employers to broaden the range of employee benefits to include dependent-care assistance as part of their standard benefits packages.

Benefits in the form of on-site day care, seminars on coping skills for families, and dependent care referral information services are usually extended to full- and part-time employees. Other benefits such as subsidized parking, employee discounts, employee assistance programs, and tuition reimbursement for job-related course work may be harder to come by if you work part-time. And executive perks like company cars and club memberships are decreasing in the corporate world and are very seldom available to part-time employees.

Compensatory Benefits

Paid leaves allow you to take time off without jeopardizing your job security. The most common types of leave are: vacation, sick, personal, holiday, maternity or parental, military, jury duty, and bereavement. Prorated leave days are most frequently available to part-time employees who work 20 or more hours a week; they are rarely available to those who work less. However, it is not uncommon for part-timers to receive no paid leave at all regardless of the hours they work.

Vacation and Sick Leave
Since most vacation and sick leave policies are based on an accrual system, they are prorated according to the number of hours worked.

Holidays
If a holiday falls on the day you normally work, you will either get the holiday paid or be expected to make up the day.

Maternity and Parental Leave Policies
With few exceptions, paid maternity benefits are left to the discretion of your employer. You'll be paid all or part of your salary while you're out on maternity leave if you have a short-term disability policy or if you have accrued annual leave and sick days that you can use during a maternity leave. If you're part of a collective bargaining unit, check with your union representative for special provisions regarding maternity leave.

Up to twelve weeks of unpaid leave is available to eligible employees under the federal Family and Medical Leave Act, which went into effect on August 5, 1993. Also, the District of Columbia and a number of states have family leave laws that, in some instances, exceed the entitlements of the new federal act.

The Family and Medical Leave Act

The federal Family and Medical Leave Act protects your job in the event you're absent from work due to the birth or adoption of a child, a serious illness in your immediate family, or recovery time needed for your own serious illness. Employees cannot be excluded from the law if they meet minimum eligibility requirements. Major provisions of the act are:

- All employers that have fifty or more employees within a 75-mile radius must comply with the law.
- Employees may take up to twelve weeks of unpaid leave following the birth of a child or upon the placement of a child for adoption or foster care; to care for a seriously ill child, spouse, or parent; or to recover from one's own serious illness.
- Employees are required to give thirty days' notice for anticipated leaves for birth, adoption, or planned medical care.
- Employers may require an employee to provide medical certification to verify a serious illness.
- Employers are required to continue health-care coverage during the leave period but they may seek to recover those payments if the employee decides not to return to work.
- Employees who wish to reduce their work schedules may be required to transfer temporarily to an equivalent position. Equivalent pay and benefits are guaranteed.
- Employees are guaranteed the same or an equivalent job when they return to work.
- Employers can exclude employees who have not worked at least one year and who haven't worked at least 1,250 hours in the previous twelve months.
- Employers may deny reinstatement to key employees, i.e., those in the highest 10 percent of the work force, if allowing the leave would cause a "substantial and grievous injury" to the business.
- Employers can substitute a worker's accrued paid leave for any part of the twelve-week period of family and medical leave.
- Employees are not eligible for unemployment compensation while on leave.

Benefits Checklist

Use the following list as a guide in determining the benefits you need and the potential cost to you if they are not provided by your employer.

Insurance Plans—Provided and paid for at the employer's discretion; employee is usually asked to share in expense.

Medical care
Dental care
Life insurance
Short-term disability
Long-term disability

Retirement Plans—Provided at the employer's discretion.

Defined benefit pension plan
Deferred profit sharing
Employee stock ownership
Money purchase pension
Other

Leave Benefits—Paid leaves, usually granted at the discretion of your employer. (Take into account lost wages if you're not paid for any time you take off.)

Vacation leave
Holiday leave
Sick leave
Personal leave
Jury duty
Military leave
Bereavement leave
Paid maternity leave
Paid paternity leave

Now that you've had the opportunity to explore the different ways flexibility can fit into your career—and your budget—it's time to move into action. Part 3 will show you how to structure your own alternative work arrangement. You will find out how to redesign your current job for more flexibility, how to write a strong proposal, and how to negotiate the arrangement you desire. And once you have your new schedule in place, we offer advice on making the new arrangement work.

TO SUM IT UP

✔ The trade-off for having more time is usually making less money.

✔ Full-time work options have no effect on the amount of salary and benefits you're entitled to.

✔ Size up your financial picture before you sacrifice salary and possibly benefits to work part-time.

✔ Don't underestimate the value of employee benefits; they're usually a significant part of your total compensation package.

✔ Employers must pay Social Security, Medicare, worker's compensation, and unemployment insurance for every employee, regardless of the number of hours they work.

✔ Paid leave and insurance and retirement plans are offered at the discretion of your employer.

PART 3

Finding Flexibility Where You Work

CHAPTER 5

STEPS TO REDESIGNING YOUR JOB

Nice work

if you can

get it and

you can get it

if you try.

— *Ira Gershwin*

Ten years ago, it may have never occurred to you to approach your boss about a flexible work schedule. Chances are he or she wouldn't even have known what you were talking about. Requesting a part-time schedule would have raised eyebrows and the thought of working from home was virtually unheard of. Your choices were simple: either you stuck it out in your 9-to-5 job or you quit.

Fortunately, times are changing. Today it is the rare employer who has not heard of telecommuting and job sharing or has not had to respond to an employee's request for a flexible work arrangement. As a record number of women, single parents, and two-career couples make up the American work force, employers are coming face-to-face with the problems and challenges of managing a diverse group of workers. No organization is exempt. Public and private employers, small and large alike, are being forced to rethink how, when, and where their employees work. These changes are opening up new scheduling options in the workplace.

Redesigning your job to match your needs with those of your employer can be a challenging and rewarding experience. It's a task not to be taken lightly and deserves careful consideration and attention on your part.

Our first piece of advice is: Don't be afraid to ask. Many redesigners we've spoken to have been surprised to find that their employer was more receptive than they expected. And our second piece of advice is: Remember that success doesn't happen by accident. Assume a "can-do attitude," create a strategy for yourself, and persevere.

In this chapter we'll help you get started on your job redesign. In the first part, we take a look at the advantages of flexibility to you and your employer, highlight the prevailing practices and attitudes employers have concerning flexible work arrangements, and alert you to some of the obstacles you may encounter. In the second part we lay out a six-step approach that we know from first-hand experience will give you the best shot at success.

FLEXIBILITY CATCHES ON

There are no national statistics on the actual number of people redesigning their jobs, but anecdotal evidence clearly suggests that the pace has picked up in the last several years. We're continually surprised at the number of people we hear about who are creating flexibility in their jobs. We meet them everywhere—at the playground, at the gym, at business meetings, and at dinner with friends.

These redesigners cross all occupations. They include accountants, attorneys, career counselors, computer specialists, engineers, health-care providers, lobbyists, public relations specialists, secretaries, and word processors, just to name a few.

We're hearing more about flexibility in the media, too. Once the staple of women's magazines, the work/family theme has become a popular topic in the national press. The *Wall Street Journal* runs a weekly column titled Work and Family, and national magazines such as *Fortune, Newsweek,* and *Time* routinely feature articles on how employers and their employees are grappling with the work/family dilemma.

Sally Wile is a classic example of someone who didn't look any further than her own job when she decided to work part-time after her daughter was born. As a Pastoral Care Coordinator for the Visiting Nurse Association, a hospice program in New York City, Sally was feeling stretched in all directions. "After two years of counseling patients and their families, I wanted to cut my schedule back to three days a week and reorganize my responsibilities to have more time for program planning," she says.

But Sally's job needed full-time coverage. Team meetings, visits to patients in three boroughs, and a never-ending pile of paperwork kept her more than busy. She decided job sharing might be the way to go. Sally started the search for a partner by tapping into her network of other ministers but in the end found the most compatible partner in Rabbi Jeffrey Marker. Now Jeff and Sally share patient care and administration in Brooklyn, Queens, and Manhattan. Sally works three days and Jeff works two and a half, overlapping one-half day to attend a weekly staff meeting. Sally's happy to have more time for program planning, and the hospice gained an unexpected benefit in the job-share arrangement when it was able to provide better services to a large Jewish population.

ADVANTAGES FOR YOU

If you're like Sally—everything about your job suits you except the hours you work—then you're a good candidate for redesigning your job. After all, why give up something you enjoy doing? Your own job may be the best place to look for flexibility in today's competitive job market.

Besides liking the work you do, there are practical reasons to stay where you are. Two obvious ones come immediately to mind: continued income and job security. If you're making a decent salary, you may want to think twice before giving it up. Your chances of making the same or better money with a new employer are slim. And as a permanent employee already on board, you're in a better position to negotiate a favorable benefits package if your new arrangement involves reducing your hours. You may also do yourself a favor by staying if you've invested a good deal of time and money toward retirement.

Other less tangible but equally important advantages we've heard about from redesigners are increased job satisfaction and a greater sense of accomplishment. "I find I can be more enthusiastic about my job because I'm not doing it every day," claims Robyn Cooper, a recruitment specialist who works three and a half days a week for a placement firm in Des Moines, Iowa. "I'm able to see things from a better perspective because I don't have to deal with the same things every day. Also on the days I'm not in the office, I have time to catch up on reading professional journals and newsletters, which helps keep me current in my field," she adds.

Joan Tyler, a research writer who works two days a week from home and the other three days in the office, finds being away from distractions of the office a boost to her creative spirit. "The biggest difference is in the quality of my work. I've always been a high producer, but creative work often requires time to think about an issue and find an interesting angle," she says.

Most part-timers will testify that a shortened workweek has made them more productive. "Better organized and more focused on the task at hand," is how Sue Sommers, a contracts administrator, sums it up. And Tracy Keeter, a former project manager for a defense contractor whom you met in chapter 3, expresses the sentiments of many part-timers: "Part of the beauty of the arrangement is that I never take time off from work for things like getting my car fixed or taking my kids to the doctor. I always know I have time for these errands on the days I'm away from the office. There's no down time for me," she says.

But increased productivity isn't the only advantage part-timers see in their flexible arrangements. In an effort to prove to their employer that their arrangements can work, many of the people we've spoken to have found themselves developing new skills. For Susan Cork and Martha Plesett, sharing the director of human resources position for an insurance firm has reaped unexpected benefits. Both feel they've grown personally and professionally. "We've become better team players," says Susan, "and I've learned to take more of a leadership role in my projects."

Upgrading management and communication skills is another by-product of using a flexible schedule. Rebecca Harding, an environmental analyst for a consulting firm in Dallas, Texas, discovered that working part-time taught her to delegate more. "It forced me to learn to use support people more effectively. I used to think it was easier to do it myself. But now I ask more of other people, give them more responsibility, and find they respect it," she says.

Gail Cooper is another part-timer who feels she's gotten a lot more out of her arrangement than she ever expected. A recruitment specialist for an accounting firm, she says, "I found I became much better at communicating with my boss and co-workers once I started working three days a week. I realized I couldn't assume they always knew what I was doing and saw that it was up to me to keep them informed."

ADVANTAGES FOR YOUR EMPLOYER

Employers also have a lot to gain by agreeing to flexible schedules for their employees. "One of the most difficult parts of doing business is finding good employees," says Erich Ohlssen, corporate director of human resources of the Adam's Mark Hotels in St. Louis, Missouri. He believes that once an organization has identified top performers, it's in their best interest to accommodate them when their personal situations change. "A modern manager must examine the demographic context in which he or she is doing business," he continues. "It becomes a matter of goal integration; you look at the needs of the individual and the needs of the organization and find an arrangement that works for everyone."

Retaining high-quality employees is at the heart of most flexible arrangements. Several major studies in the last five years have shown that holding on to valued employees outranked all other reasons for employers offering flexible work options. In a 1989 survey conducted by Catalyst, a national research and advisory organization in New York, 68 percent of the companies reported retention as the most significant advantage of using flexible schedules.[1] Two years later, a 1991 survey by the Conference Board, a business and economic research organization in New York, reinforced this finding: Fifty-six percent of the respondents viewed retention as a motivating factor.[2]

Erich Ohlssen put his theory into practice when he went to bat for Suzanne Bortin and Shelly Tsipori, the first pair of employees at the hotel to request a job-share arrangement. "They're both absolutely first-rate salespeople, long-term employees who had a very substantial record of success and achievement behind them—all the indications that would make this a beneficial arrangement were there, so it just made sense," he explains.

Joanne Gage, vice president for consumer affairs at Golub Corporation, knows what a valuable employee she has in Maureen Murphy, a home economist who has worked part-time for the last four years. "Maureen does everything from nutrition education programs to market research. We use her for anything and everything," says Joanne. "She has a long history in the department, is well-rounded, knows the people within the company, and presents herself very well. With this and her ten years of experience here, I get as much out of her in two days a week as I would out of a full-time person with less experience," she adds.

Sharon Alfred Decker is another example of a manager who has used flexible scheduling to her company's advantage. Faced with the combined challenge of improving employee relations and the customer-service functions of ninety-eight local offices for Duke Power Company in Charlotte, North Carolina, Sharon turned to a variety of work schedules as a way to improve employee morale and performance. By doing away with swing shifts and instituting four 10-hour days and three 12-hour days, she cut attrition to 12 percent annually in a business where 40 percent is the norm.[3]

Boosting productivity and commitment to the organization is another bonus for managers who offer flexible schedules to their employees. Most of the evidence supporting increased productivity was scant until the Families and Work Institute, a nonprofit, New York-based research organization, released the results of two studies in 1993. They measured the impact of flexible schedules on employees at two companies: Johnson & Johnson, the world's largest health-care products company, headquartered in New Brunswick, New Jersey, and Fel-Pro, an auto-parts manufacturer in Skokie, Illinois.

Results of the Johnson & Johnson study found absenteeism among their employees using flexible schedules to be 50 percent less than that in the rest of their work force. The study also reported that 58 percent of the employees surveyed rated the availability of such programs very high in their decision to stay at the company. The results of the Fel-Pro study showed a strong link between job performance and the use of flexible schedules, stating that employees using flexible schedules have some of the highest job performance and are least likely to leave the company.

A direct link between productivity and telecommuting spawned U S WEST's interest in that option. John Scott, area manager of work-site alternatives at U S WEST, views the company's telecommuting program as a "win-win situation" for both the employer and the employee. He says the increase in productivity comes when employees are able to work during their most productive time, even if that's 3:00 in the morning.

WHY YOUR BOSS MIGHT SAY NO

Attitudes and policies regarding flexible schedules vary greatly from one organization to the next. Although there are promising signs everywhere of employers creating more options in the workplace, we would be remiss if we left you thinking that redesigning has become the status quo. We frequently hear about people who shy away from pursuing a flexible schedule for fear they'll either lose their job or be held in less esteem.

Much of this opposition to flexibility comes from middle management. Managers who stand in the way of accepting flexible work options often feel such options conflict with standard business procedures. Others who have always done things in a certain way find a safe haven in the traditional 9-to-5 workday. Whatever the reason, they fail to see flexibility as an important employee issue and are philosophically opposed to getting involved in their employees' lives. Most of all, the mere suggestion of trying something new sends them running for cover.

Our experience, along with that of many others, indicates that the greatest resistance centers around part-time and work-at-home arrangements. Holding on to traditional beliefs that professionals working part-time lack commitment, that telecommuters are not team players, and that job sharers cost too much has inhibited many managers from endorsing these options. Other stumbling blocks that cause them to reject flexible work arrangements include misconceptions such as:

- **Everyone will want to do it.** Many employers cling to the myth that if one person works part-time, the floodgates will open and they'll be inundated with similar requests.
- **Productivity will drop off.** Getting beyond the psychological hurdle that if employees can't be seen, they must not be working has prevented many a manager from approving a flexible arrangement for an employee.
- **Flexible workers aren't committed employees.** Bosses who manage by the concept of face time—that is, the amount of time spent at work determines dedication to the job—have trouble seeing part-timers as committed employees.
- **Headcount will be upset.** The traditional system of allocating human resources in which one person, regardless of the amount of time worked, is counted as one employee, gives managers little incentive to consider part-time positions. Even in companies that have done away with the headcount system, it's hard to get long-time managers to think otherwise.

- **Loss of control.** Managers used to being a desk away from their staff worry about how they'll supervise at-home workers.
- **Flexibility increases costs.** Many employers perceive additional administrative and benefits costs. While there might be additional costs associated with job sharing or telecommuting, they are usually minimal.
- **Flexible work options aren't for professionals or supervisors.** Many employers still believe that flexible work options are only suitable for those in low-level positions and jobs routine in nature.

Despite some of these pitfalls or others you might encounter, don't be discouraged. There's plenty of common ground for you and your employer to meet on. Half the battle of restructuring your job is believing you can do it and then thinking creatively about how to make it happen. While employer philosophy and practice are not to be discounted, how well you present yourself will tip the scales in your favor when it comes to getting final approval.

PLANNING YOUR STRATEGY

A question we're often asked is: "When should I start planning to make a change?" Our answer invariably is: "It's never too soon." But in reality we know that most people don't think about it until they have a pressing need. The more time you give yourself, the better your chances are of fitting a flexible arrangement into your career.

Debbie Rhoades, a nutrition and education training specialist with the Maryland State Department of Education, said it best: "From day one I started to make myself indispensable to my boss. I knew the day would come that I'd want to work part-time and I planned to give her every reason to say yes."

Barbara Wahlbrink, who has worked in sales and marketing for a Fortune 100 company for ten years, took a different but equally effective approach. She recommends you concentrate on developing contacts through-out the hierarchy of management before you request a part-time schedule. "If you have the luxury to plan ahead, make your network as broad-based, as deep, and as wide as you can, because getting support from all levels of management is very helpful when proposing a flexible arrangement in large companies."

Whether you have the luxury of planning ahead or you're faced with making a move on short notice, you'll need to build a persuasive case that's going to get you the yes you want to hear. Use the following step-by-step process to help you design your new way to work. It's worked for others, and we feel sure that it will work for you, too.

SIX STEPS TO REDESIGNING
YOUR JOB

What does redesigning mean? Simply put, it's the process of adjusting your job responsibilities to match your schedule change. The amount of adjusting will depend on the complexity of your job and the option you choose.

For example, if you plan to continue working full-time in a compressed workweek or flextime arrangement, your schedule will need minimal reworking. Telecommuting, on the other hand, requires careful planning to sell your employer on the idea of working all or part of your time at home. And the challenge of redesigning your job to fit a part-time schedule is finding the right blend of responsibilities that draw on your strengths and are of greatest value to your employer.

Step One: Choose a Work Option

The first task in designing a new work schedule is to take a close look at your needs, both personal and financial. Decide what it is you really want to accomplish. If you hope to have more personal time by cutting back on your hours at work, can you live with the financial compromises you might be forced to make? If not, what type of flexible full-time schedule will give you the time you need? Is working at home a feasible alternative to consider? Do you see this change as a temporary solution or long-term arrangement? If it's long term, are there career trade-offs to consider?

At this point it's important to hone in on a work option that meets your needs. At the very least, decide between working full-time and part-time. Once you've made that decision, focus on the option that appeals to you. If you're still not sure which route to take, refer back to chapter 2 for a discussion on the features of each option.

Step Two: Gauge Your Employer's Commitment

There's no universal formula employers use when they offer flexible work schedules. You'll find policies in the private sector run the gamut from formal to ad hoc arrangements. In fact, a 1989 survey by Catalyst showed that only 25 percent of the companies surveyed had formal policies with guidelines for implementing them, and more than 61 percent reported having no formal policy at all.[4] The prevalence of formal policies is often a factor of company size. Generally it's the larger companies who view flexible work options as part of their work/life agenda and have incorporated them into their personnel policies. Smaller organizations lean more toward the ad hoc arrangements.

Even when you find flexible schedules included in the personnel policy, they're not necessarily available in all departments or to all employees. You may find supervisors and managers are excluded, or you may find yourself transferring to another department in order to get the work arrangement you want. And endorsement from the top doesn't automatically guarantee you'll get support from your manager, explains Barbara Wahlbrink. "The company may have a part-time policy and be very supportive publicly, but it's still a local management decision. And in most cases, management is not very supportive, even though corporate policy allows it," she says. Barbara's experience is not an uncommon one for people working in large organizations. Many companies have policies in place but do little to encourage their use.

If you work for a government agency, you'll find less variation on flexible policies. Regulations exist on the federal, state, and local levels, but usage varies widely. And again, the ease of using one of these arrangements will depend on the agency's implementation of the regulations and your supervisor's attitude.

Before you approach your supervisor, find out about your organization's flexible policies. Start by checking your employee handbook or with your personnel office to see what the policies and practices are. And, if you belong to a labor union, be sure to check out its position regarding flexible work schedules. If there's no formal statement, check around to find out what's been done "informally." As you do your research, look for answers to the following questions:

- Does your organization offer the full range of full- and part-time options, or is it limited to just one or two options, such as flextime and telecommuting?
- Are flexible work arrangements included in the personnel policy? If so, are all employees (i.e., support staff, technical assistants, and supervisors) eligible to participate? Or are certain departments or groups of employees excluded?
- How many others in your organization use flexible schedules? What departments or types of jobs seem to make the greatest use of flexible arrangements?
- Has top management publicly endorsed the use of flexible schedules? If so, has their support filtered down the ranks to front-line supervisors?
- Are flexible schedules limited to employees currently on the payroll, or are they also extended to new hires?
- If your organization doesn't have flexible work policies, does it show an awareness by supporting other work/family initiatives, such as providing child and elder care information and referral services, working parent support groups, and counseling for work-and-family related problems?
- Have women left the organization following maternity leave because they were not granted a flexible arrangement?
- What happens to your salary and benefits if you reduce your hours? This may serve as a good indication of your employer's attitude toward part-time.
- Does the company provide training programs for employees using flexible schedules? Is training also offered to their supervisors?

Step Three: Decide Who Decides

Sometimes the route to approval is straightforward. In other cases, it's hard to get a handle on who will be making the final decision. Most likely your immediate supervisor will have the final say—at least he or she will have to agree to it—but it's not uncommon for proposals to be sent up the chain of command and subjected to two or three levels of approval. This is especially true if you work for a large organization or a government agency.

If your boss isn't making the final decision because he or she won't or can't, find out who is in control. Put on your politician's hat to figure out who you'll need to convince to start lobbying on your behalf. It may be your boss's boss, a regional manager, or the senior vice president for human resources. When Barbara Wahlbrink realized her local manager was hesitant about approving her part-time request, she suggested meeting with the regional manager, who knew her and her work. She sold the regional manager on her request, who in turn sold it to the vice president of the East Coast region.

Marianne Kilgore, whom you'll hear more about in chapter 7, had a similar experience when she proposed cutting back her work schedule from five to four days a week. An attorney with a state legal department, her boss was not prepared to sign off on the arrangement but agreed to give it a try if his boss approved it.

Step Four: Draw on the Experience of Others

Talking to others can be a morale booster as well as give you insight into what's worked for some and what hasn't worked for others in your organization. You're likely to get the best advice from someone in a job and work arrangement similar to the one you're proposing.

Sue Bishop, an economic policy analyst with a nonprofit think-tank, attributes her success in getting a part-time schedule to the pointers she received from Denise Carpenter, a senior project manager in another department of the organization. "Denise was a tremendous help when it came to figuring out how to sell the idea to my boss. Her insights into management's biases helped me focus on points that would counter their concerns," Sue explains.

Anticipating possible resistance from her boss, Margaret Fox, an executive secretary at a mid-size insurance company, got a few good tips from talking to two other part-timers in the company. Both administrative assistants, their supervisors had expressed some of the same concerns as Margaret suspected her boss would—lack of phone coverage, availability for special meetings and conferences, and just being there whenever he needed her.

"I was able to get another secretary in the division to answer phones for me the day I was off as long as I would cover for her one day a week. In addition, I agreed to be available to help with meetings and conferences, even if it meant switching my day off occasionally," Margaret says. Using some of the strategies suggested by her co-workers, she was able to allay her boss's fears from the start.

Learning from the experience of others will save you time and help you anticipate problems that hadn't occurred to you before. If you're a trailblazer in your organization when it comes to flexible work schedules, seek advice from someone within your industry working in a like job with a similar schedule.

As you talk to others, look for answers to the following:

- Which flexible arrangements have been or are currently being used in your organization? Do they include clerical, technical, and professional positions?
- What has made them successful and what aspects have caused problems?
- What strategy did they use for dealing with the chain of command? Did they solicit support from other managers, former supervisors, or the human resource manager?
- Do they feel like "second-class citizens"? Have they lost their job title or prime office space? Have they been excluded from office social functions, been the butt of snide remarks, or in other ways received unfair treatment?
- Have they remained eligible for raises and promotions?

Step Five: Take a Realistic Look at Your Job

This is the most important step in the process, yet the one most often overlooked. If you lack a clear understanding of how the demands of your job will fit into your proposed arrangement, you run the risk of not getting the job done to your satisfaction or to that of your employer. Your goal should be to preserve the essence of your job. Give high priority to keeping the responsibilities you excel at, those that give you the greatest satisfaction, and those that are most important to your employer. Here are some suggestions to keep you on track.

Start by keeping a log of your daily activities, preferably for one month. Although this may seem tedious and unnecessary, it'll give you a much better idea of where and how you're spending your time. It will also ensure that you don't overcommit, in other words, take on more than you can reasonably do under your new schedule. Be sure to include the occasional breakfast meeting, work-related social obligations, and the time you spend working on the weekends or in the evening at home.

List the tasks you do and the amount of time you spend on each. Rank them according to importance—from highest to lowest priority. Note those aspects of the job only you can do, and those which, conceivably, could be done by someone else in your department. If you're considering a job share, this is a good time to think about how you plan to divide up the work load. And if you're in a supervisory position, you'll want to take a careful look at how you'll handle these responsibilities under your new arrangement.

As you look at your job, ask yourself the following questions:

- If you want to work part of your time from home, does your job include such tasks as reading reports and publications; or writing papers, newsletters, and manuals, or producing financial analyses that could easily be done away from the office?
- Does your job require working at more than one location, i.e., a satellite facility, client's office, or "on the road"? Will this hinder or benefit your proposed arrangement?
- Do you routinely work overtime? Is it required or are you a "workaholic"? Are you prepared to scale back?

- Is your job portable? Do you rely on equipment, paper files, and reference materials only available at the work site?
- Is face-to-face time important in your job? How much contact time you have with managers, peers, support staff, colleagues in other departments, clients, and customers?
- If your job includes supervisory or management responsibilities, what changes will you be required to make to continue in this position?
- Are there specific days or times of the day you must be available at work, i.e., for staff meetings?

Step Six: Size Up Your Leverage

A big selling point when you redesign your job is your years of service with the organization. As a seasoned employee you understand the ins and outs of the job, you know the players and their personalities, and you're familiar with your employer's operations and programs. And hopefully, you're known as someone who can get the job done. All this adds up to an indisputable track record that will give you an edge when you're ready to negotiate a new work arrangement. Indeed, we've heard first-hand from redesigners and their employers and know from our own experience that having a reputation as a valuable employee is the most important ingredient to a redesigner's success.

Barbara Wahlbrink sums it up best when she says, "I had a fairly broad base of support in terms of people I knew and people who knew my performance on projects. I think that was a key to working out my new arrangement." Kathryn Luther, a geologist who works for the North Dakota Health Department Water Quality Division, agrees: "I felt the key to converting my full-time position to a job share was a proven record of high-quality work with the department."

But having a good track record may not go far enough. You may also need to focus your employer on other qualities that set you apart from the pack. Do you have a hard-to-find skill, special expertise, or an entrenched relationship with important clients? These attributes make you nearly indispensable.

Judy Beechly, a corporate fundraiser in Chicago, found she had tremendous leverage with her employer because she alone had developed a network of corporate contributors over an eight-year period. She knew her boss would be hard pressed to find someone to step into her shoes without putting some contributors at risk.

Jane Lyder, an attorney with the U.S. Department of Interior, found her length of service to be an advantage. Her fifteen years of service lends continuity to an office staffed by political appointees who change with each new administration.

In short, you'll build a convincing case by zeroing in on the things that give you leverage:

- years of service
- a good reputation
- recognition throughout the organization
- people like you
- cost savings if your employer can retain your expertise or experience but pay you less if you work part-time
- extra benefits for the company, such as institutional memory, extended office coverage, availability during peak times, or increased flexibility in meeting various work loads or new projects

Now that you've worked through these steps, a lot of the work is done. You're ready to move on to the proposal stage.

TO SUM IT UP

✔ Redesigning your job can reap unexpected benefits for you and your company.

✔ Don't be afraid to ask. Your employer may be more receptive than you think.

✔ Be aware of your employer's objections.

✔ Good planning on your part is essential.

✔ Find out how committed your employer is to flexible work arrangements.

✔ Zero in on the decision maker.

✔ Preserve the essence of your job.

✔ Use your leverage to your advantage.

CHAPTER 6

WRITING A WINNING PROPOSAL

If you fail

to plan, you

are planning

to fail.

— *Anonymous*

Y ou've done the groundwork. You've decided on a work option that will give you the greatest satisfaction personally and professionally, collected information on your organization's attitude about flexible work arrangements, and made a realistic analysis of your job. Now you're ready to take your plan to the next stage: writing a winning proposal that will persuade your employer to approve your new arrangement.

If you have a boss who is open-minded and receptive to the idea of flexible work arrangements, you may not have much trouble getting your new work schedule approved. As a matter of fact, you may find that a well-timed meeting is all that is needed. In this case, your written proposal serves as confirmation of your discussion. However, in most other cases, a proposal lays the groundwork for the next step of negotiation.

In this chapter we'll take a look at choosing the best time to approach your boss, writing an effective proposal, and determining the merits of suggesting a trial period. You'll find some sample proposals at the end of the chapter; use them as a guide, altering them to suit your style and your organization.

TIMING IS EVERYTHING

Choosing the right time to present your proposal to your boss can make or break the deal. Our advice is to approach your supervisor informally before submitting your request in writing. You're the best judge of what time is most favorable for both of you. It may be a point of discussion you bring up at your annual review or at a regularly scheduled appointment. However, if you're accustomed to talking things over informally, don't change your approach. A chance encounter or raising the issue over a cup of coffee may be the best way to let your boss know what you have in mind.

An informal discussion serves a number of purposes. It gives you a chance to "float" the idea before you put it in writing, it's an opportunity to size up your supervisor's attitudes, and it may tip you off to some of the obstacles you're likely to encounter. Don't be discouraged if your supervisor is hesitant about your plan. You can address his or her concerns in your written proposal. Proceed by suggesting a time for a second meeting after your boss has had the opportunity to review your written plan.

A word of caution: The office grapevine is not how your boss should hear about your plan. Use discretion in discussing it with co-workers until you've talked to your supervisor first. Maintaining a good relationship with your boss throughout your negotiations is paramount since she or he will either have the final say on your proposal or be asked to make a recommendation up the chain of command.

When Do You Raise the Question?

How far in advance of your arrangement should you approach your boss? The answer to this question depends in part on your own needs. Do you have an urgent situation that requires adjusting your work schedule immediately? Are you planning for the time when you return to work following parental leave? Or do you have several months before you need the new schedule?

While planning well in advance of your desired start date is generally preferable, you may not have that luxury. If your needs are pressing, suggest a temporary arrangement. You can refine the details and discuss making the new schedule permanent later on.

In some instances you may find your supervisor unwilling or unable to commit to your request too far in advance, as Maura Ragner, a senior planning specialist with a federal agency, discovered. "I knew returning to work full-time following the birth of my second child was out of the question," says Maura. "What I didn't know was when to raise the issue with my boss. Given the staffing changes in our division, I had to think carefully about when I thought my chances were best. I finally decided I wanted the issue resolved prior to going out on leave."

Two months before she was scheduled to begin her leave, Maura approached her boss about cutting back her work schedule to 30 hours per week when she returned from her three-month leave of absence. "I thought by giving my boss enough notice she could plan accordingly. However, she didn't see it that way. Anticipating budget cutbacks, she felt uncomfortable planning that far in advance. Clearly, I asked too early," Maura notes.

As Maura entered the final month of her leave, she felt pressed to finalize her plans for returning to work. While on leave, Maura had kept in touch with several co-workers, who let her know that her boss was under a lot of pressure. "Since I already had spoken with her on several occasions, I decided the best approach this time was to submit my request in writing. Although it took her the full month to respond, I feel putting the request in writing paid off," explains Maura. After her leave of absence, Maura's request was granted: She returned to work on the 30-hour-per-week schedule she wanted.

Whatever your timetable, there are certain periods to avoid: budget reviews, major project deadlines, staff reorganizations, or any time you know your boss is under considerable pressure. One of the best times to approach your supervisor is when you've been recognized for good work performance, completed a project successfully, or in some other way distinguished yourself.

"Working long hours on a major project kept me from bringing up the subject," says Leigh Carver, "but the day my boss and I had lunch to mark the successful completion of the Davidson project I knew that I was in a good position to raise the issue of cutting back my work schedule to 24 hours a week."

Leigh, a management analyst at a mid-size company, notes that "although this was a first-of-a-kind request, I felt my chances were pretty good. About a week after our lunch, I presented my plan to work on Mondays, Wednesdays, and Thursdays to my boss. She thought the idea was doable and asked me to submit a proposal outlining the details."

Leigh didn't run into any resistance from her boss. However, if she had raised the issue in the middle of trying to complete the Davidson project, her boss's response might have been lukewarm at best.

PUTTING IT IN WRITING

Are written proposals necessary? Definitely. A well-organized written proposal protects your interests and has a better chance of being approved than an oral request. As one human resource manager put it: "It shows you've thought through the details of the arrangement."

A written proposal:

- helps organize your thoughts clearly;
- increases the chance of a response from your boss;
- avoids misunderstandings on both sides;
- allows you to address potential problem areas and offer solutions;
- ensures all aspects of the arrangement are considered;
- guarantees your perspective is presented accurately if your proposal is taken to upper management by someone other than you;
- provides documentation of the arrangement should there be a change in management; and
- gives you confidence to approach the negotiating table with a positive attitude.

Style and Format: Tailoring the Proposal to Your Situation

The first impression is the most lasting. Your proposal should look like any other proposal you would present to management—professional in appearance, orderly, and to the point. If it looks good and reads well, you're one step closer to getting a favorable response. In some cases, your proposal may serve as the formal written agreement or contract signed by you and your employer.

Take into account the style of communication in your organization, policy requirements of your company, and the chain of command reviewing the proposal when putting your thoughts together. If your immediate supervisor is the only one approving your request, your proposal can be less formal and less detailed than when a more senior manager must approve it.

The language in your proposal is important, too. Keep it simple, unemotional, and nonthreatening. Avoid comments such as "If this arrangement is not approved, I will be forced to resign." Such statements raise a red flag to management; they bring up questions about your commitment to your job and are likely to jeopardize your chances for negotiating a suitable arrangement.

Written proposals range from an informal one-page memo to a more formal multipage document. Choose a format compatible with the type of change you are requesting. The more complex the change, the more detailed your proposal is likely to be.

A short, simple memo was sufficient for Jim Crane, a single parent of two young girls and a research scientist, when he requested a flextime schedule allowing him to start and finish his workday earlier than his colleagues so that he could be home to meet his daughters' school bus.

Similarly, a short memo will probably suffice if you're proposing to compress a full-time, five-day workweek into four days, or if you're requesting a flextime schedule. In these cases, your proposal should highlight concerns that might arise from your absence during "regular" business hours, such as your availability to clients and for staff meetings.

On the other hand, if you're planning to reduce the total number of hours you work, either through a regular part-time arrangement or a job share, your proposal will need to be more comprehensive and detailed.

"Our proposal turned into a rather lengthy document," said Pat Holloway, as she reflected on the work that went into drawing up a plan to share the directorship of the Southeastern Connecticut Library Association with a co-worker. "We broke the job into three main areas: financial, office oversight, and travel. For each of the three areas we outlined in detail how we would divide up the responsibilities," comments Pat.

POINTS TO COVER IN YOUR
PROPOSAL

The most effective proposal will include the salient points of your arrangement and anticipate concerns your supervisor might have with it. If you're suggesting extensive changes to your job, your proposal should include the following elements:

- introduction
- proposed work schedule
- advantages to your employer (see also cost savings below)

- availability issues
- redefinition of job duties
- salary and benefits
- cost savings
- performance evaluation
- trial period
- supporting information

We suggest the above order, but it's not the only one that works. You may be able to build a stronger case by highlighting the cost savings or by suggesting a trial period up front. Be sure to omit those points that don't apply to your situation.

Keep in mind that the degree of detail required in each section will vary according to the work arrangement you are proposing. If you're making minor changes to your schedule, you may only need to include the first four points. On the other hand, if your proposal stretches into a multipage document, consider attaching a cover letter summarizing the important points of your proposal. Also, if you are looking for a quick response from your boss, the cover letter is a good place to mention it.

Introduction

As we said earlier, the first impression your supervisor has about your request is the most important one. A clear, concise statement about why you are proposing a change in your schedule will improve the chances of your request receiving full attention. Give one reason for wanting to change your schedule, such as "to accommodate family responsibilities" or "to be available to care for aging parents" or "to reduce commuting time." Remember, your manager is not interested in the details of how long your commute is or what a hassle it is to get your kids off to daycare or school. She or he also doesn't want to get a shopping list of activities you have planned for the time you're away from the job. Frame your reason in a way that presents you as a serious, responsible worker with a commitment to your career and to the job.

Proposed Work Schedule

Describe your proposed work arrangement by including the number of hours per day and per week you plan to work. For example, if you are proposing to work part-time, your schedule may be Monday through Thursday, 8:30 a.m. to 3:30 p.m. Indicate when you want your arrangement to take effect, and how long you anticipate it will continue, i.e., six months, one year, or for an indefinite period of time.

If you're planning to job share, outline the schedule of both partners, including overlap time if that's part of your arrangement. If you're proposing to work at home part of the time, indicate which days you plan to be in the office and which ones at home. Be sure to include the schedule for your work hours at home if it varies from your organization's official work schedule.

Advantages to Your Employer

Employers want to know what's in it for them. Use this section to demonstrate persuasively the advantages your employer will gain from your proposed arrangement. Be specific when showing how your expertise and knowledge of the job make you a valuable asset your employer can't afford to lose. Some advantages might include:

- Retaining an experienced and skilled employee. Employers keep down their recruiting and training costs by retaining workers who are experienced and know the company's programs and policies.
- Reduced absenteeism and employee turnover.
- Greater productivity. Employees who use flexible schedules are generally more productive because they are less fatigued and stressed and tend not to use work time for taking care of such things as doctors' appointments and other nonwork needs.
- Increased flexibility in meeting various work loads or new projects.
- Reduced burn-out. Flexible working hours can provide time to recharge energy and motivation, especially in high-stress jobs.
- Personnel coverage during extended business hours. This might be the case if your new schedule would mean you're working before or after normal business hours.

Availability Issues

One of the biggest concerns expressed by managers about flexible schedules is that there is less face-to-face contact. If your proposed work arrangement involves a significant rearranging of work hours, change in workplace, or reduction in work schedule, you need to come up with a system for maintaining contact and continuity with the people you work with both inside and outside your workplace.

You can head off potential problems and make it harder for your boss to turn down your request if you have thought through some of these trouble spots ahead of time and have outlined procedures for dealing with them.

Use this section of your proposal to describe how you will handle potential availability issues. They might include how you plan to deal with:

- scheduled and unscheduled meetings
- project or publication deadlines
- client needs
- staying in touch with co-workers
- follow-up activities, such as reports and phone calls
- emergency situations or urgent calls

Redefinition of Job Duties

If you're only changing your place of work or the arrangement of your full-time hours (compressed workweek, telecommuting, flextime) you can bypass this section. On the other hand, if you're proposing to reduce your hours so you can work part-time or share a full-time job with someone else, both you and your supervisor need to have a clear understanding of how this change will affect the specific duties and responsibilities of your job.

Making substantial changes to your job (i.e., eliminating specific tasks or adding new ones) may require writing a new job description. If you find yourself faced with giving up certain parts of your job, be sure to keep the responsibilities you find most desirable and those that make you most valuable to your employer.

For the job duties you're proposing to relinquish, suggest how they will get done. You may want to recommend reassigning work you'll no longer personally handle to a more junior co-worker or suggest hiring another part-timer to pick up the slack. We've even heard of a case where the job duties of a whole department were realigned, which satisfied several staffers in the end.

If you're in a management job, outline how you will delegate work to your staff. And if your position requires travel, state your continued availability for short- and long-term trips.

If you plan to job share, detail how the job responsibilities will be divided up. You may find that you and your partner take equal responsibility for getting every task done, or you may find there is a clear-cut way to divide up the duties. Most importantly, don't leave loose ends for your employer to tie up.

Sandy Laval, a full-time attorney in a corporate legal department, took the latter approach when making a convincing argument for redesigning her position into a job-share arrangement:

"I knew there was no way my job could be done on a part-time basis, but since my work load was split evenly between litigation and administrative work, it was perfect for a job-share arrangement," Sandy explains. "One of us could concentrate on court appearances and the other on compliance reviews and training field staff. Since it was a logical way to divide up the work, my supervisor was willing to give it a try. In the end he got two very energetic employees who were highly productive and unlikely to burn out from the high stress and pressure of the job."

Salary and Benefits

Proposing a flexible full-time option—flextime, compressed workweek, or telecommuting—should have no impact on your pay and benefits package because you are still working the standard number of hours.

However, if you're considering a reduced work schedule—part-time or job sharing—your total compensation package will change. Use this section of the proposal to show how your salary and benefits will be affected by your proposed arrangement.

Generally, the best strategy is to suggest prorated pay and benefits. For example, if you're proposing to reduce your work schedule by two days or 40 percent, then on a prorated basis you will receive 60 percent of your current pay. If you're a salaried employee and your job involves irregular hours or overtime, you may want to recommend that comp time or an hourly rate be established so that you're compensated for all the hours you work past your regular schedule.

Unfortunately, the benefits issue is not as straightforward as the salary one. Company policy may determine which benefits you're entitled to as a part-timer and the basis on which they are calculated. If so, state the policy in your proposal. In the absence of an official policy, suggest a prorated package based on the number of hours you work. Refer back to chapter 4 for an overview of what can happen to your benefits if you work part-time.

Cost Savings

Employers are always looking for ways to save money. Use this section of the proposal to detail the savings your employer will realize if your request is approved. Examples are savings from salary and benefits, if you are reducing your work hours, and overhead expenses such as office space, if you are working from home.

In the case of a job-share arrangement, your employer may incur additional costs related to payroll taxes and benefits. Social security taxes will be slightly higher if your salary is above the maximum taxable wage, and unemployment insurance will cost your employer twice as much. These details aren't usually spelled out in a proposal, but you need to be aware of them. The cost of benefits will increase only if both job-share partners receive more than half the standard benefits package. In your proposal, spell out the benefits you and your partner want. However, it's to your advantage to focus on the cost savings of the arrangement.

When Pat Holloway teamed up with a partner to share the director job at the Southeastern Connecticut Library Association, they devised a highly customized benefits package that met their needs and saved their employer money. "The association was paying between three and four thousand dollars for benefits for each full-timer. Our combined benefit allowance of twenty-eight hundred dollars came in well under that," Pat says.

Fortunately, Pat and her partner each had health insurance coverage through their spouses, because even if they had wanted to enroll in the plan, Pat says, "The company that provides our health insurance doesn't allow part-timers to participate." As a result, Pat and her partner proposed an alternative plan that was approved. They each ended up with the same package, which included: a two hundred dollar reimbursement toward an annual medical check-up, a two hundred dollar reimbursement toward a life insurance policy, a one thousand dollar match toward an IRA fund, all paid leave days prorated to 70 percent, paid holidays when they fell on the day they worked, and twelve days of annual leave.

Performance Evaluation

Whether you're working full-time or part-time, in the office or at home, it is important to remember you are entitled to regular performance reviews, raises, promotions, and, in some cases, bonuses. If your proposed arrangement involves a change in the duties and responsibilities of your original job, now is the time to spell out and agree on a new set of performance criteria against which your work will be evaluated. If you're recommending a job-share arrangement, decide at this stage if you'll be evaluated individually or as a team.

Trial Period

Suggesting a trial period is advantageous to both you and your employer. It provides you with an opportunity to fine-tune your schedule or adjust the work load you committed to once you've had a chance to test the arrangement. The trial period should be long enough to give you, your boss, and your co-workers time to adjust to the new schedule before it is evaluated.

Leslie Scherer, who shares the director position with Karen Roesler at the Wallingford Public Library in Wallingford, Connecticut, says: "A four-month trial period gave the library board, town officials, staff, and the general public a chance to react to dealing with two people at the top, and we both had a chance to see how comfortable we felt with the arrangement, too." Karen adds: "In the end we needed to make some significant adjustments, but they were well received by the board since we had built in an evaluation period from the beginning."

A trial period can be a powerful inducement to convince a reluctant boss to approve your plan. By proposing a graceful way out of the agreement, you've given him or her a good reason to test your plan.

Dana Quinn, a marketing representative for a pharmaceutical firm, used this strategy when she proposed working from home two days a week. Her request was something new for the company and her manager was concerned that her absence from the office meant reports wouldn't be turned in on time and she wouldn't be available for staff meetings.

"Between two hours of commuting a day and visiting my accounts, I was always on the road and had no time to get caught up on my paperwork," explains Dana. "Since several of my major accounts are located within 10 miles of my house, I proposed calling on them the days I worked from home, using the rest of the day for phone calls and follow-up paperwork." Initially, Dana's supervisor was reluctant to approve her request, but finally he agreed to a six-month trial period. "After two months he came to me and said he was pleased with the way the new arrangement was working out," she is happy to report.

Supporting Information

Managers generally prefer to adopt practices that have been proven to work. Your case will be stronger if you can provide examples of other employees in your organization who have successfully used the arrangement you are proposing. Include information on where it has been tried and with what results. Remember, the basic proposal should be clear and concise. A long written document could discourage a manager who is already wary of a complicated plan that requires changes and rethinking on his or her part.

If you're a "pioneer" in your organization, cite examples of similar organizations in your area that make flexible schedules available to their employees. Make sure the examples are appropriate and support the kind of change you are suggesting. This information can be incorporated into your proposal unless it becomes too lengthy. In that case, you may want to include it as an addendum.

One of the best resources for finding out what other companies are doing is your local library. Today, most public libraries have computers that let you access articles on a variety of data bases. Use a key word or phrase such as part-time, job sharing, or telecommuting to conduct your search. The computer will identify for you magazine and newspaper articles that address the option you've chosen. If your local library can't help you, try a college or university library in your area.

The business section of your local newspaper is another good source, as is the Sunday *New York Times* and the weekly Work and Family column in the *Wall Street Journal*. *Working Mother* magazine features family-friendly companies regularly in its October issue. (See Appendix C: Further Readings for a list of articles and books on flexible work arrangements.)

Attachments to your proposal might include any or all of the following:

- a list of other companies that are using the arrangement you are requesting
- copies of reports discussing the pros and cons of flexible work options
- newspaper and magazines articles featuring the use of various flexible arrangements
- short bibliography of information available on related issues

SAMPLE REDUCED WORKWEEK PROPOSAL

MEMORANDUM

To: R. J. Waller
From: Stacy Sullivan
Date: May 30, 1993
Subject: Reduced Workweek Proposal

As we've discussed, attached is my proposal to implement a six-month reduced workweek pilot program as a training specialist. This proposal will give me the flexibility needed to meet both my career and family goals.

Among the benefits to ABC Company, Inc., is the retention of a ten-year employee with a proven track record and experience in computer training.

I appreciate your interest and am available to discuss this proposal at your earliest convenience.

Stacy Sullivan
Training Specialist
ABC Company, Inc.

Introduction

This proposal for a reduced workweek schedule will enable me to continue my career goals and balance my work and family life. The first three months will give me time to complete my final project for a master's degree in training and development prior to finalizing the adoption of a child. Thereafter, I would like to continue my part-time arrangement under the Dependent Care program.

Proposed Work Schedule

I propose to work three days per week: Tuesday, Wednesday, and Thursday. I would follow normal ABC Co. work hours of 8:30 a.m. to 4:30 p.m. for a total of 24 hours.

Advantages to ABC Co.

The main advantage to ABC Co. is the retention of a ten-year employee with a successful performance record in computer training who has in-depth knowledge of the organization and operations of ABC Co., knowledge of current computer technology, and expertise in designing and developing training programs for major marketing computer systems.

Secondly, as the Systems Training Department moves into technology-based training, it is critical to establish a solid expertise base for the ongoing design and development of training programs. I believe this can best be accomplished by maintaining a permanent staff familiar with the needs of the organization, rather than the current practice of hiring people on an as-needed basis. Allowing me to use a reduced workweek arrangement would fit into developing this long-term stability and strategy for the department.

REDUCED WORKWEEK PROPOSAL, CONTINUED

ABC Co. is clearly interested in working with the changing and challenging issues of a diverse work force as articulated in its employee publications and through its work/family programs. This proposal provides ABC Co. an opportunity to support its commitment and test the feasibility of a flexible work arrangement in the training department.

Job Description
The following assignments are suitable under a reduced workweek schedule:

- Implement and maintain a technology-based training center.
- Provide instructional design expertise on training projects to ensure sound instructional design methods are used in developing systems training.
- Research, recommend, develop, and implement on-line documentation and performance support systems for various departments.
- Conduct classroom training for various systems.

Availability
The proposed three-day-a-week schedule will give me enough "face time" to interact with support staff and still be available to lead training sessions on a regular basis.

Using e-mail and AUDIX, ongoing communication should not be a problem. I plan to check for messages on the days I'm not scheduled to work.

The training schedules at ABC Co. would remain unchanged since most training is scheduled for Tuesdays through Thursdays.

Trial Period
This proposal is for a six-month pilot project to determine the feasibility of a reduced workweek in systems training. At the end of that time, an evaluation will be made for continuing this work schedule for an indefinite period of time or for returning to work full-time.

Performance Evaluation
A reduced workweek would not require any change in the current personnel performance system. Performance will be based on specific objectives that have been set to be completed during the six-month trial period.

Salary and Benefits
The terms of this proposal would be the same as the Dependent Care Reduced Workweek program with pay and benefits prorated.

Supporting Information
ABC Co. currently offers a Dependent Care Leave of Absence and Reduced Workweek program for a period of up to six months. I understand from Corporate Employee Relations there are several situations in which longer-term arrangements have been made based on the individual situation and departmental requirements and approval.

For example, there are several employees in the Facilities Department who work a variation of the reduced workweek or who work at home. Marketing at the A&B Center has just extended a work-at-home situation, and in the Professional Services Group the Dependent Care Reduced Workweek has been successfully utilized by several employees.

Sample Job-Share Proposal

MEMORANDUM

To: John Jones, Human Resources
From: Barbara Nelson and Connie Mathews
Subject: Job-Share Proposal
Date: June 4, 1993

We, Barbara Nelson and Connie Mathews, would like you to consider our proposal to job share the crucial breaking news shift at XYZ Network. We think this shift lends itself to a job share since each workday is self-contained; as a general rule, segments are booked and produced on the same day with little carryover.

We propose a starting date of July 1, 1993, and recommend a one-year commitment, with an evaluation period at the end of the first six months.

We believe sharing our job would be good for us and for XYZ. We feel at this time in our lives a part-time schedule would give us more time for our family responsibilities and would also give us more energy for our job. We believe XYZ would benefit from this arrangement for the following reasons:

- Retention of valuable employees. Two experienced, skilled, and proven employees who together have a total of nine years under XYZ policies and guidelines and a total of twenty-four years in the news business.
- Job continuity. The availability of two experts to provide continuous coverage.
- Wider range of experience. Two experts bring two sets of contacts, two Rolodex card files, and a broader perspective to the job. For example, one producer specializes in politics and the arts; the other producer specializes in features and social trends. Both share experience in hard news, sports, and technical television production.

- Good public image. The company makes a major public relations statement as a forward-thinking company regarding changing work-force demographics and increasing focus on the family.

Schedule
We propose to split the workweek evenly, each of us working three days. Barbara Nelson's work schedule would include Sunday, Monday, and Tuesday. Connie Mathews will work Wednesday, Thursday, and Friday.

Division of Duties
We both have worked in this position for several years, know our jobs well, and believe this shift lends itself to sharing since each workday is self-contained. As a rule, segments are booked and produced on the same day, keeping spillover from one day to the next at a minimum. This makes the changeover with a partner very easy.

In addition to covering news stories during the week, Barbara Nelson will be "on call" Sunday and will spend her time on Sunday researching for the week ahead, booking any breaking news segments, or booking Monday segments as needed. Connie Mathews's duties on Friday include covering morning tapings, researching stories for the week ahead, preparing weekend stories, or booking ahead Monday segments.

Communication Plan
We plan to share an office with interchangeable coverage of phone calls and mail throughout the week. We will maintain contact by telephone and use electronic messages when necessary. We will be in daily contact with the executive producer and fellow producers while in the office. Staff meetings will be attended by the job sharer working at the time of the meeting, unless the manager requests that both job sharers attend. We will meet together on a monthly basis or as needed to discuss and review the needs of the job.

Office Set-up

We plan to use one office and one telephone and to keep one budget and time account. Our business entertainment expense account will not exceed that of one full-time employee.

Performance Evaluation

As a team we will be jointly accountable and share responsibility for the total job, and, therefore, we would expect to be evaluated together on this basis.

Salary and Benefits

Since we are each working 60 percent of a full-time schedule, we propose that salary and benefits be prorated accordingly. We propose to retain our staff employee status with all rights to insurance and saving plans kept intact. Because we both will be continuously employed, we will retain seniority rights.

Other Issues

If one job sharer decides to leave the job-share arrangement, the remaining job sharer will have the opportunity to present another candidate to management for approval.

Thank you for your time and consideration of this proposal. We feel positive that job sharing will work in our situation and look forward to receiving your answer.

TO SUM IT UP

✔ Time your request favorably for you and your employer.

✔ Tailor the style and format of your proposal to your situation.

✔ Use convincing and persuasive language in your proposal.

✔ Focus on the advantages to your employer.

✔ Follow up an informal conversation about your proposed work arrangement with the details in writing.

✔ Provide a system for handling availability issues.

✔ Show how the work you will no longer be doing will be handled.

✔ Suggest a trial period.

CHAPTER 7

NEGOTIATING A NEW WORK ARRANGEMENT

Never let us

negotiate

out of fear.

But let us

never fear to

negotiate.

— *John Fitzgerald Kennedy*

At its best, negotiating is an art and with good reason—two sides engage in a well-crafted discussion to end up with something each wants. Negotiating a flexible job is really no different. It's likely you and your employer will go back and forth until you hammer out a deal that suits both your needs.

Despite this give-and-take, we have one sure-fire piece of advice about negotiating. You'll have the best chance of getting what you want if you have a positive attitude and you're well prepared with a written proposal.

In this chapter we'll give you pointers on how to negotiate a new work schedule and job responsibilities, and for part-timers, how to keep your salary and benefits intact. We'll also tell you how to handle special situations such as employer resistance and offer strategies to keep in mind once you sit down at the negotiating table.

Negotiating a new work arrangement can take one short meeting or may stretch into months, depending on the following factors: the degree of change to your schedule and job duties; the level of cooperation or resistance from your boss; the number of people who must approve your arrangement; the experience of others in your organization; and the nature of policies and practices affecting the decision-making process.

Take Sarah Wellman and Alessandra Tyler, for example. They are both public relations managers but at different nonprofit associations. Each wanted to convert her full-time job to part-time following a maternity leave.

"When I was seven months pregnant," Sarah says, "I approached my boss with a written proposal on a Tuesday morning and had a yes by the end of the week." Alessandra had an initial meeting with her boss in her eighth month of pregnancy and presented her proposal a week later. "Over the next five months I negotiated my proposal with three layers of management. The week before I returned from my maternity leave, my request was finally approved," she explains.

Sarah had an unusually easy time of working out a new arrangement; Alessandra's negotiations were more complicated and perhaps more the norm. In fact, conversations with our colleagues suggest that you should be prepared to attend several meetings to agree on the details of a new arrangement. A lengthy negotiation may take every ounce of persistence and patience you have, but it's worth it to end up with a schedule you and your employer can live with in the long run.

Tips for Negotiating Your Proposal

Negotiating is the ability to satisfy the needs of another party without compromising your own position. Keep the following points in mind before negotiating your work arrangement with your employer:

- Be aware of your mutual interests. Your negotiation should result in meeting your needs and the needs of your employer.
- Act with integrity and be honest when you negotiate your proposal.
- Be prepared. Go into the negotiation knowing exactly what you want and what your employer has to offer to reach your goal.
- Decide on your range of negotiation. The range is the difference between what you want and what you're willing to accept.
- Be realistic. Setting goals that are too high may cause an early deadlock, but setting goals that are too low will sell yourself short.
- Your leverage is your negotiating power. Be aware of your strengths and use them aggressively as bargaining chips.
- Keep emotion out of your discussions. Negotiate on the merits of your proposal.
- A successful negotiation is marked by two parties who both feel they have won.

GETTING READY TO NEGOTIATE

Before you head to the negotiating table, look for clues from your employer about how she or he is likely to handle the negotiation. Here are some questions to ask yourself:

- Were preliminary discussions you had with your boss positive or strained?
- Is your boss inclined to do anything to keep you, or are you easily replaceable?
- Is your boss a stickler for details?
- Is your boss slow to change or does he or she want to be seen as progressive and in touch with the needs of the staff?
- Has your boss been supportive of you in the past?

Many managers new to workplace flexibility are likely to move slowly on approving requests. Arm yourself with examples of how the schedule you want has worked for others and be specific about how you plan to make it work for you. Try to keep your manager focused on the advantages of your plan and suggest a date by which you need a response.

Draw on the experience of others in your organization in similar positions who have negotiated a flexible schedule but don't be limited by their results. You may be in a stronger position to negotiate a better deal if your skills are more marketable, the terms of your proposal are more desirable, or you're simply a better negotiator and more effective in getting what you want.

Finally, ask a friend, relative, or trusted colleague to role-play a mock negotiation with you. This will allow you to practice responding to the tough questions and will help build up your confidence for the real thing. In a later section in this chapter you'll find some sample questions to use in your mock negotiations.

You'll be ready to sit down at the negotiating table when you've resolved the following:

- You know how you're going to get the job done in the work schedule you've proposed.
- You've identified the advantages to your employer.
- You know what your leverage is and you're ready to use it.
- You're prepared to counter your employer's concerns.
- You feel ready and confident to move forward.

Experience Pays Off

Jim Ketcham-Colwill, who proposed a flexible full-time schedule to his employer, used his years of experience as a bargaining chip in his negotiation. When their first son was born, Jim and his wife decided they would both work four days a week so he'd only be with a sitter a few days each week. For his wife, an attorney with the Environmental Protection Agency (EPA), negotiating a flexible schedule was fairly straightforward. For Jim, it wasn't quite as easy.

"I raised a lot of eyebrows when I went to my employer asking to work a four-day week," says Jim. At the time a staff writer for a congressional caucus that published a weekly newsletter, Jim felt he had the perfect job to convert from five to four days a week. A weekly newsletter deadline kept him at the office until very late many Friday evenings, but Mondays, a notoriously slow day, seemed a logical one to stay home. "Considering the extremely long days we put in on Fridays, I'd still be putting in over 40 hours a week even on a four-day schedule," he explains. "I knew I could meet my deadlines and promised right up front to get the job done."

Despite this logic, his employer had reservations and feared that everyone would ask for a compressed schedule if they let Jim have one. Jim had two long conversations with his manager over a period of a few weeks. In his meetings he emphasized that he wanted to be a father more than just on weekends and that he was committed to his wife's desire to have a career.

Convinced that a flexible schedule was very important to Jim and wanting to keep a good employee, management approved his request after a month. As a condition of the arrangement, Jim also agreed to work late every Friday night, instead of on a rotating basis with his co-workers, to meet the weekly deadline.

Jim's years of experience were clearly a plus, which he worked to his advantage. His employer also saw his willingness to work every Friday night as a fair trade for having Mondays off.

NEGOTIATING JOB
RESPONSIBILITIES AND SCHEDULE

When you negotiate your arrangement, appear accommodating to your boss's needs without giving up the flexibility you want. You may be forced to make a few concessions along the way, but in the end, both of you should be comfortable with the terms of your new arrangement.

If you're continuing with a full-time schedule or you're reducing your hours by 15 percent or less, the responsibilities of your job probably won't change much. However, if you're reducing your schedule by more than 15 percent, be prepared to convince your boss that the job will get done. The following points will help you stay focused when discussing the details of your proposal:

- Stand firm on keeping the tasks that make the best use of your talents and that you enjoy doing the most.
- Don't commit to more work than you can handle on your proposed schedule.
- Ask for a commitment from your employer that you'll continue to have the same level of responsibility on projects and assignments.
- Offer suggestions for covering the work you will no longer do, such as reorganizing staff, hiring a part-time employee, or streamlining the way the work is done.
- Suggest that you relinquish lower-level work you've outgrown to a more junior staff person.
- Be firm on the schedule you suggest, but if your boss has reservations about it, be prepared to discuss how you'll finish your work in the time proposed.
- If your boss is suggesting a different schedule than the one you proposed, push for a trial period to prove how your plan can work.

Ann Portman, a designer with a small engineering company, is a good example of someone who successfully negotiated a new work schedule. When she presented her proposal for a part-time schedule to her boss, she wanted to work three 8-hour days: Monday, Wednesday, and Thursday.

"My boss had no trouble with my working a 24-hour week because we had already agreed that I would service fewer clients, but she was really uncomfortable with the idea that I'd be out of the office two days a week," says Ann. Her boss suggested she work Monday through Friday, 5 hours a day, which Ann found less appealing. "Finally," Ann says, "We compromised on four 6-hour days, Monday through Thursday. For me, it was a doable schedule and I considered it a small compromise for staying in a job I really enjoy."

Other important points to discuss include your availability for phone calls, meetings, and out-of-town travel on days you're not scheduled to work, as well as supervisory duties if you're in a management position. If you travel to meetings and conferences, have heavy client contact, or if your boss and co-workers are used to relying on you for advice or help on a daily basis, consider the following points before you negotiate your availability during the hours or days you're not scheduled to work.

Telephone Calls

Decide to what extent you'll be available to handle phone calls during the times you're not working. Be realistic. If you'll be home caring for young children, unexpected phone calls may be a nuisance.

- Offer a plan for handling important calls when you're not available, such as asking a colleague to respond to urgent calls.
- If you plan to selectively return phone calls when you're not working, define which ones you're willing to take.
- If you plan to work from home, negotiate with your employer to pay or share in the cost of phone services, such as voice mail, call waiting, and call forwarding. Be prepared to justify the expense and show how they'll make you a more effective long-distance worker.

Persistence Pays Off

One of six attorneys for a state government legal department, Marianne Kilgore spent five months negotiating a part-time schedule. Marianne first approached her supervisor, Keith Whitley, in March asking to work part-time by reducing her schedule by 5 hours a week. She says, "I was turned down immediately because there was a chance one of my co-workers would be taking a medical leave of absence and we were expecting a few big cases in late spring."

Even though Keith rejected her request, he said he might consider it in the future. When it became apparent that Marianne's co-worker was not taking a leave of absence, she went back to Keith a second time in late May, this time avoiding the phrase "part-time" and asking for a "slightly reduced" schedule. She also suggested they try out the schedule for the summer, delaying a permanent decision until after Labor Day.

When Keith failed to get back to her, she decided to put her request in writing. Marianne recalls, "Before I had a chance to present my proposal, Keith wrote me a memo with the heading 'Re: Your Request to Have Fridays Off for the Summer and Indefinitely.' He said he couldn't approve my request because he was uncomfortable with it. Keith thought everyone would want to work part-time and that my schedule would mean more work for him. He was also hoping to get another attorney slot funded and felt it might be denied if he had a part-time attorney on board." Even though Keith did not approve the schedule, he said he was willing to try it if his boss, Randy Thornton, signed off on the idea.

The following morning Marianne asked Randy for a short meeting. Once she laid out her plan, Randy said, almost immediately, "I see no problem with it. I'd love to work that schedule myself."

(continued on next page)

(continued from previous page)

Before giving her final approval, he discussed Marianne's request with Keith and confirmed the decision with the court administrator.

Marianne kept emotion out of her request and treated it as a business transaction. Her patience in negotiating her proposal up the chain of command, even seizing the opportunity to go over her immediate boss's head once he gave her the green light, was the key to her success.

Meetings

Decide to what extent you'll be available for meetings that are scheduled for the times you're not at work or when you're working from home.

- If coming into the office at unscheduled times is a problem, suggest that you "attend" important meetings by conference call.
- If you agree to attend emergency meetings in person or by phone, do you want to be compensated for the extra time worked?

Travel

If business travel is part of the reason you want to change your schedule, be prepared to explain how you will still do your job without traveling as often or how goals associated with trips can be met in other ways.

- Decide on the extent of travel you'll be available for.
- If you plan to travel, agree that travel will be planned in advance.
- Request the flexibility to change your work schedule around the weeks you travel.
- If travel increases the hours you work in a week, do you want to be compensated? If so, how?

WHAT IF YOU'RE A SUPERVISOR?

Managers and supervisors who want to work a flexible schedule themselves often face an uphill battle as they try to convince their employer it can work. If you think your proposed schedule will allow you to continue managing a staff and you wish to do so, negotiate hard to hang on to these responsibilities. In the long run, you'll have a better chance of protecting career advancement opportunities and keeping your earning power intact if you continue in a leadership role. Unless your employer has a written policy prohibiting supervisors from using flexible schedules, don't assume you must give up managerial responsibilities when you alter your working arrangements.

If you find your employer reluctant to approve your request, reiterate the points in your proposal, stressing how your management style is compatible with your proposed schedule. For instance, it's a plus if you've built a trusting relationship with your staff and they're used to handling the work you delegate to them.

When Catherine Griffin, an account executive with a cosmetics firm, negotiated a schedule to work 32 hours a week, she assured her boss her arrangement could work because of the way she ran her department. She said, "I told him my staff was used to accepting responsibility because I'd always operated under the assumption that they were up to any task until they proved otherwise. I had also planned ahead by giving them more access to our clients so they'd feel comfortable with making decisions." By giving specific examples of how her staff could carry out their work independently, she sold her boss on the idea of a part-time job.

Pat Spellman's story is another good example of how to make and win your case. When Pat was negotiating a compressed workweek schedule, she was ready with an answer when her boss asked her what her staff would do without a supervisor every Friday. Pat says, "He was immediately disarmed when I reminded him that my job had always required travel and meetings that took me out of the office, and that I had handled it by keeping in touch with my staff by phone, faxing them instructions in the morning, and sometimes requesting a faxed progress report at the end of the day. By having an answer ready, I dealt with the issue firmly and it never came up again."

NEGOTIATING YOUR COMPENSATION

For many, the biggest hurdle in reaching a satisfactory arrangement hinges on the impact a changed schedule has on pay and employee benefits. This only comes into play if you reduce your hours from full-time to part-time or you set up a job-share arrangement. If your employer has firm policies in place regarding salary and benefits for part-timers, you'll have little or no negotiating room.

On the other hand, if your organization has no policies regarding flexible schedules, and you're the first one to pursue a part-time job, you may have a better chance of negotiating a favorable package. Whatever the situation, aggressively pursue the best salary and benefits package your employer has to offer.

Pay

Our first piece of advice is: *Don't* take a pay cut. But do agree on an equitable method of calculating your pay. If you're a salaried employee, you can remain on salary or go to an hourly wage. The downside of converting your salary to an hourly wage is that you may lose your benefits because many companies don't pay benefits to part-timers on an hourly wage. The upside is it may be easier to be compensated for any extra time you put in.

Keep in mind the following points when you negotiate pay:

- Maintain your current rate of pay. If you're paid a salary, it should be prorated according to the number of hours you work. If you're paid an hourly wage, the rate should stay the same.
- A prorated salary works best if you know you'll be working the same number of hours every week.
- An hourly rate is desirable if the number of hours you work regularly fluctuates, requiring you to put in extra hours on the job or at home.
- If you're a salaried employee putting in a lot of extra time, negotiate additional pay or consider comp time.
- If you're accustomed to receiving bonuses and other financial incentives, you should remain eligible to receive them.

Benefits

Every part-timer we talked to wants to keep benefits and nearly every employer we know wants to take them away. Clearly, benefits is one of the most difficult issues to negotiate. Unfortunately, escalating health insurance costs and pressures on employers to cut overhead are making it tougher for part-time employees to remain eligible for the same benefits enjoyed by their full-time co-workers. Before you negotiate the specifics of your benefits package, refer back to chapter 4 for more information on employer policies and practices.

When there's no clear-cut company policy, it may be advantageous to negotiate insurance coverage, paid leaves, and retirement plans separately. For instance, health insurance may be a non-negotiable benefit if your organization's carrier doesn't allow part-timers to participate, but paid leaves are offered totally at the discretion of the employer and should be aggressively pursued. Prorated sick and vacation leave should be the minimum you receive in your negotiated benefits package. And keep in mind that pension plans vary widely from employer to employer.

Remember the following points when you negotiate your benefits:

- Hang on to as many benefits as possible. Once you lose them, they're nearly impossible to get back.
- If your organization has a policy regarding benefits for part-timers, study it carefully beforehand so that you know what's fair game when it's time to negotiate.
- If you lose your benefits, negotiate more salary to compensate for the cost of insurance coverage you'll have to get on your own.
- If your employer has a pension plan for all employees and you work 1,000 hours (an average of 20 hours a week) or more a year, under the federal Employee Retirement Income Security Act (ERISA), you're entitled to participate.
- Consider working more hours a week if it will qualify you for benefits.

Creative Benefits Negotiating in a Job Share

Shelly Tsipori and Suzanne Bortin's story is a good example of how one job-share team resolved the difficult issue of negotiating benefits with their employer.

When Shelly and Suzanne proposed sharing Suzanne's catering manager job at a hotel in Philadelphia, their need for benefits nearly doomed the negotiation. Since their husbands are self-employed, they both wanted a paid health insurance plan. With this priority in mind, they proposed working 20 hours a week each and asked for full benefits plans and prorated salaries. Their immediate supervisor and the general manager of the hotel were supportive of their request, but the executives at headquarters had their doubts.

Shelly recalls, "They were reluctant to set a precedent and voiced concerns about clients being confused by dealing with two of us, but the biggest issue for our employer was giving both of us paid benefits."

Eager to have their arrangement approved, Shelly and Suzanne each offered to work 30 hours a week, which meant that one of them was at the hotel every day, seven days a week. They also increased their joint sales goal by 20 percent. Together, these features easily compensated for the added cost of a second benefits package.

Shelly and Suzanne were wise to look for creative solutions to a management concern that might have jeopardized their proposal. Negotiating an arrangement that offered two advantages to their employer—consistent coverage for the catering functions on weekends and increased sales—proved to be a winning combination.

WHAT CAN HAPPEN TO YOUR PERKS

WHEN YOU WORK PART-TIME

Perks, which is short for perquisites, are the extra benefits you receive when you're in a management or executive job. You won't find them spelled out in a personnel handbook, and they may be handed out rather arbitrarily by the powers-that-be, but they speak volumes about your status in the organization.

They're not just the "little things," but important trappings of success, such as an assigned, and perhaps free, parking space; access to the executive dining room; use of a corporate credit card; paid memberships at private dinner and health clubs; and the most sacred—a windowed office.

The people we interviewed expressed their strongest feelings when they recounted experiences of losing their perks. Tracy Keeter, who was forced to relinquish her manager's role once she started working part-time, explains, "When I went to a part-time schedule, I was demoted from life. I couldn't believe it when I lost my parking space and was no longer allowed to eat with my colleagues in the executive dining room."

Losing a windowed office seemed to hit most people the hardest. Often yanked out from beneath them on a day they didn't work or while they were out on maternity leave, this unwelcome change caught them totally off guard. Jill Ferrin, a scientist in Oregon, told us she knew she'd have to make concessions on the type of research projects she would be assigned to when she started working part-time, but she was unprepared for losing her private windowed office, which was taken away from her without warning. She says, "I'm relieved to at least share a windowed office. If I should lose that, it would be the most devastating thing about working part-time."

If you suspect you may lose some of the perks you've been used to getting, you may want to mention them during your negotiations. However, it's best to save this conversation for the end of your talks, once your employer's convinced he or she needs to keep you.

Pitfalls to Avoid When Negotiating Your Arrangement

- Don't apologize for requesting a flexible schedule.
- Don't act like your boss is doing you a favor by "letting" you redesign your job.
- Don't threaten to leave or quit; a hostile tone won't get you positive results.
- Don't start your negotiations by giving your benefits away.
- Don't compromise beyond the limits you set for yourself.

COUNTERING YOUR EMPLOYER'S
OBJECTIONS

Even in the best of circumstances your boss is likely to have reservations about doing things differently. Many of the people we interviewed faced the same barriers when they approached their employers about using flexible work arrangements. It seemed to matter little what line of work they were in or if they had large or small employers: The reactions from their employers were much the same.

We have included the employer reactions you're most likely to run into and our suggestions for an appropriate response. These should give you an idea of how to handle yourself if you're in a similar situation. Note that the tone of your answer should be positive but firm, and never threatening.

Your employer says: "If I let you work part-time, everyone else around here will want to, too."

You say: "It may sound good to a lot of people but, when it comes down to it, not everyone wants to work part-time or can afford to take the pay cut."

Your employer says: "If you're working from home two days a week, how will you be able to give your clients the service they're used to getting?"

You say: "I'll be just as available to my clients from home as I am from the office. I rely on voice mail and call forwarding now, I'll just use it more frequently."

Your employer says: "What will your staff do if you're gone every Wednesday?"

You say: "I trust my staff. They're used to working independently when I'm out of the office at meetings or traveling. They always know how to reach me and I usually call in once a day."

Your employer says: "Your slot is going to cost me a lot of money if I let you job share."

You say: "We'll be sharing an office and all of our equipment. Administrative costs of having two people on the payroll are minimal and we're splitting one benefits package down the middle. We think it's a good investment since we can cover for each other when one or the other is on vacation or out sick."

Your employer says: "How will I know what you're doing if you work at home?"

You say: "I'll be responsible for the same work that I've always done and for meeting the same deadlines. The only difference is that I'll be doing it from home a couple days a week."

Your employer says: "How about travel? I really need you to attend the meetings I've been sending you to."

You say: "I can still do most of that. When I can't go, I'll send one of my staff. A few of them are ready for the opportunity and have asked for more responsibility."

Your employer says: "I'm not sure our clients are ready for someone who's only working part-time."

You say: "I prefer to be discreet about my work arrangement. Unless there's a good reason a client must know about my schedule, I don't see any reason to tell them."

Your employer says: "How will we file our Friday afternoon reports on time if you leave at 3:00 p.m.?"

You say: "I'll have time early in the morning before anyone else is in to write my portion of the reports. If it doesn't work out, I won't flex my hours that day."

Your employer says: "No one's ever done this before. I don't think it can work."

You say: "I've thought my plan through carefully and believe it will work out just fine. Let me try it for a few months to see if we can work it out together."

Your employer says: "Personnel will never buy this. You know how resistant they are to trying something new."

You say: "I know it's a new idea, but I'm prepared to sell my proposal to anyone who needs convincing. I hope I can count on your support."

WHAT TO DO IF YOU'RE

TURNED DOWN

Unfortunately, a negotiation doesn't always result in a meeting of the minds. If you find yourself in that position, find out why your request was denied. In any event, don't give up! You may have a few more avenues open before you make a decision to stick with your current situation or leave the organization. Here are some other options to consider:

- Create a new job to fill an unmet need in your company.
- Choose a different work option that answers your employer's concerns. For instance, if your boss is convinced your job can't be done on a part-time basis, consider job sharing or perhaps working some of your time at home.
- Try again at a later date. Your proposal may look more reasonable to your boss once a major project is finished or at the start of a new fiscal year.
- Look in another part of your company for a job that lends itself to the schedule you're proposing.

■ In the end, if the answer is still no, accept the decision graciously. No matter how disappointed you may be, don't do anything to put yourself in disfavor with your boss or the company. More than likely you'll need them for a reference one day. Even if you leave at this point, you may wish to return in the future.

TO SUM IT UP

✔ Approach the negotiating table with a positive attitude.

✔ Prepare yourself to negotiate by sizing up your bargaining chips.

✔ Highlight the advantages of your plan to your employer.

✔ Be specific when negotiating your salary, benefits, and schedule.

✔ Don't negotiate your benefits away.

✔ Be ready to counter your employer's concerns.

✔ If your negotiations fail, consider a different work option.

CHAPTER 8

MAKING IT WORK FOR YOU AND YOUR EMPLOYER

To strive,

to seek, and

not to yield.

— *Alfred Lord Tennyson*

You've negotiated the flexible schedule of your dreams but that's only half the battle. Now it's time to make it work. How you handle yourself and your work arrangement is the key to making your new schedule a success. Robin Sheldrick, a recruiter in the pharmaceutical industry, said it best when she told us, "I always think it's a compliment when someone says, 'I didn't know you work part-time.' When I hear that I figure I've pulled it off."

What can you do to make your arrangement a success? There are steps you can take from day one and things you can do along the way to ensure everything runs smoothly. For starters, you may need to tinker with your schedule, your work load, or get your co-workers on board.

If you've cut back your hours significantly, your biggest challenge may be letting go of some of the work you've always done. Working at home may be a difficult change or a refreshing one, as you adapt to a new rhythm of working. And if you're job sharing, you'll be in the unique situation of making a "marriage" work while getting the job done.

Think of your actions as preventive medicine for keeping your job situation healthy and thriving. What you do from the outset will minimize your problems in the future.

MAKING IT WORK FOR YOU

Every situation is different and what works for one person isn't necessarily the answer for someone else. In the end, responsibility for making the arrangement work will rest on your shoulders. Here are some suggestions to help you get off to a good start:

Keep a positive attitude. That means that if you had to compromise on some of the terms, don't show your disappointment. If co-workers are resentful, find a way to win them over, or if your boss is having a hard time adjusting to your absence, find ways to stay in touch. A positive, self-assured manner will send a clear message to your co-workers and supervisor that you can get the job done.

Be flexible and accommodating to unforeseen changes whenever possible. We've heard countless stories from people who switched work-days to attend meetings, returned phone calls to clients on days off, took on extra assignments, and worked overtime to meet an important deadline. As long as they were extending themselves as an exception and not the rule, they believed the extra effort earned them respect from co-workers and supervisors and proved their commitment to the job.

Make the most of a trial period. If a trial period is part of the deal, use this opportunity to fine-tune the arrangement. Resolve any unexpected problems that have surfaced, such as adjusting your schedule slightly to accommodate your needs or those of your employer. The time and effort on your part may make the difference between wholehearted support and reluctant acceptance.

Keep track of the hours you work. Whether you're salaried or paid by the hour, keep a daily account of the hours you work and the assignments you complete. This may sound tedious and unnecessary, but it takes little effort and can be good insurance at performance review time or if you find yourself reporting to a new manager. A record of your hours can help bolster your case if you find that you need to renegotiate your compensation because you're consistently putting in more time than you're being paid for.

Know when to say no. It's best to be responsive to your employer's needs by doing what it takes to get the job done, but sometimes there's a fine line between going the extra mile when it's important to do so and saying no. If you find yourself falling into the trap of agreeing to do more than you can realistically handle on your schedule, then it's time to set limits.

"When I started working part-time, I thought I had to do it all," recalls Marisa Wells, manager of community relations for a large company. "When I'm on the job, I'm very focused, but I had to set limits on what I could get done in three days a week. Now that I've settled into a routine that works, I've gotten over the fear of losing my job if I let my boss know when too much is too much," she says.

Be selective when telling others about your schedule. People using the greatest discretion in revealing their work schedules are part-time professionals uncertain of how colleagues and clients will react to their arrangement. One hydrogeologist told us: "I would never tell my $10-million client that I work part-time for fear he would have me taken off the project. I've trained my staff to call me immediately if he calls on my day off and I return the call by locking myself in an interior bathroom far from the noise of my two children," she recounted.

Use work time for work. Refrain from using work time to attend to personal matters, such as routine doctor's visits, personal calls, and errands, especially if you're working part-time. A conscientious approach will establish your credibility and convince others you're committed to the job.

Find flexible dependent care arrangements. If you're caring for children or sick or elderly relatives, you need backup dependent care to accommodate sudden changes in your work schedule. Some people we spoke to use home day-care providers or elder-care centers that are able to provide additional care on short notice.

Others, particularly lawyers, doctors, and executives with unpredictable schedules, regularly engage full-time dependent care, which allows them complete flexibility. This is an excellent solution for those who can afford it, however, it's an unrealistic alternative for most of us. Your schedule should be reliable enough that you don't have to resort to such an expensive measure to make your arrangement work.

MAKING IT WORK FOR
EVERYONE ELSE

If it works for you but doesn't work for your supervisor, your co-workers, and your clients, it probably won't work for you for very long. Put yourself in their places and try to understand how your scheduling changes are affecting them. Then do what it takes to make it work for all involved. Here are some places to start:

Be sure co-workers are informed about your arrangement. Co-workers can be your greatest allies. You're likely to find them far more supportive if they understand the details of your arrangement. As a first step, keep them informed of your schedule, especially if it varies during the week or from week to week. If there's not much overlap in schedules, find out when everyone is available to talk over work and keep each other on track with assignments and deadlines. You also have the best chance of being included in important meetings and getting interesting assignments if everyone knows when you plan to be on the job.

Spell out your availability when you're not working. Letting your boss, staff, and co-workers know the boundaries is important. Most of us don't mind being called at home on days off to answer a quick question or with a request to return an important call to a client, but spending several hours on a conference call, being called repeatedly throughout the day, or being asked to attend meetings on your day off more than once in a while is inappropriate unless you agree to this exception and you're compensated for the extra time worked.

Set up a system for handling phone calls. Since it's not important (and sometimes undesirable) for people outside your organization to know the details of your schedule, you need to tell your receptionist, secretary, and co-workers how you would like them to handle your calls.

For instance, people should avoid saying, "Sally is never here on Tuesdays and Thursdays." Instead they should say, "Sally isn't in today, but I expect her to return tomorrow. Unless your message is urgent, she'll return your call in the morning." In effect, the response the caller gets is really no different from the one he would get if he had tried to reach someone with a heavy meeting or travel schedule.

Take advantage of technology to stay in touch with co-workers and clients. Perhaps the best invention for people who have flexible work schedules is voice mail. Your phone is always answered, you can change your greeting as frequently as you wish, and you can pick and choose the calls to return when you're away from work. If you're electronically linked by home modem to your place of work you can keep in close touch with fellow workers by sending and receiving e-mail messages at your convenience 24 hours a day.

Fax machines are a boost for people working at home but can lead to overwork if you can't walk away from the temptation of getting just a few more letters or reports out. A part-time senior executive chuckled when she told us about the fax machine she received from her boss at Christmas. "He told me it would make my life 'easier,'" she said, "but I saw it as a thinly veiled invitation to work even more hours at home."

Consider "volunteering" for extra duty or work assignments. There are times when everyone has to pull a little extra weight to get the job done. If your department is working to meet a deadline, has a large conference to staff, or has some other unusual demand to meet, volunteer to be among the ones to stay late and finish up. The goodwill you engender will be worth the inconvenience to your schedule.

Solicit feedback from others. During the trial period, if you have one, informally ask your boss, co-workers, and staff for feedback on your schedule—what they think has worked and what hasn't. A simple question such as "Has my new work schedule caused you any problems?" may uncover difficulties or resentments that can be corrected before they become major issues.

If you do hit a snag or run into a problem with a co-worker, deal with it quickly and in a professional manner. You might ask for suggestions in resolving the differences. People who feel included in making your arrangement work will be more supportive when your schedule is evaluated for further use.

Stay in the loop socially with co-workers. If you're not in the office as much as you used to be, occasionally make time for lunch or for a drink at the end of the day with co-workers to let them know they're important to you. If you have the resources and space, offer to have the next work-related social function at your house. You'll be most successful in fending off the naysayers and those who are jealous of your schedule if you're seen as a team player.

MAKING IT WORK WHEN YOU
SHARE A JOB

If you move from a full-time work schedule to a job-share arrangement, you're facing several new challenges at once. You're cutting back on the hours you work, relinquishing parts of your job that you've always done, and learning to work in a new way with someone else. The transition may be an easy one if you and your partner have worked together before, but don't count on it.

Working together in the same job is very different from working side by side in two different positions. The job sharers we interviewed found success using the following strategies:

Be flexible. A set schedule is preferable, but be prepared to switch days off to accommodate each other's personal needs and to occasionally work extra hours to finish a project or prepare for a special event. Be available by phone to each other to answer questions or provide input on major decisions.

Don't be competitive with your partner. Recognize each other's strengths and weaknesses and work around them so you both look good.

Don't leave messes for your partner to clean up. Especially if you don't work consecutive days, tie up loose ends and return all phone calls by the end of your workday so you don't leave it for your partner to handle the next day.

Be considerate. Divvy up the fun work as well as the less desirable chores such as attending long meetings. In your partner's absence, don't volunteer her for assignments or meetings you would rather avoid.

Put a good communication plan in place. Keep each other up to speed on assignments and what's happening in the office by being available to one another by phone and, when necessary, by leaving detailed notes or memos for each other. Copy your supervisor and key staff to keep them informed.

Familiarize yourself with the work your partner is doing. Staying up to speed on each other's projects allows both partners to provide continuity to co-workers and clients. Each partner should be able to answer incoming calls and correspondence and represent the team at meetings.

Fine-Tuning Until It Works

Vicki Baldassano and Jill Tallman share a beat as staff writers for the *Pension Benefits Reporter* at the Bureau of National Affairs. In the summer of 1992, Vicki was looking for a writer to share her job at the same time that Jill, also interested in working part-time, was returning to work following a six-month maternity leave. Vicki and Jill had been in the same employee group and had the same supervisor but worked on different publications.

With all sides agreeing they had a good match, Vicki and Jill started a one-year pilot of their job-share arrangement in September 1992. Jill says, "Being in the same office and covering the same subject matter helped the success of our arrangement. Vicki didn't have to bring in anybody from a different department who wasn't familiar with the way we did things or bring in someone from outside the company."

With a weekly deadline to meet each Friday, Vicki and Jill wanted to work at least one full week at a time to provide continuity for themselves and their boss, and to minimize leaving partially researched and written stories for one another to finish. They decided the best way to split their schedule was by working in two-week cycles.

Since they're away from the office for two weeks at a time, Jill says a key to their success is communication. "We talk on the phone with each other quite a bit and we leave very detailed notes for each other at the end of our cycle," explains Jill. They also copy their supervisor on the memos they leave for one another and keep him informed in writing of their work schedules. Jill says, "He likes our schedule to be entered in a computer file so he can use it to make assignments."

(continued on next page)

(continued from previous page)

In the beginning, Jill and Vicki shared one work space, which called for a special effort on Jill's part. She recalls, "Vicki's a very neat person and I am not a neat person, so when I reached the end of my rotation, I had to go through and clean everything up, wash out the coffee cup, clean the rings off the desk, and get the fingerprints off the computer terminal." She jokingly adds, "Now I have my own space that I can leave any way I want to."

At the end of their twelve-month pilot, the job share was made permanent. They used that time to re-evaluate their arrangement and decided to reconsider their schedule. Because Jill finds it hard to get back up to speed after being away for two weeks, she proposed to Vicki that they try working on one-week cycles.

"I like working two weeks on and two weeks off so we're still negotiating over this," says Vicki. "We're going to try working one week on, one week off for one month to see how it works out. If we like it, then we'll decide whether or not to keep it."

The team is also negotiating who should work which holiday weeks. Vicki worked most of the weeks that included a holiday last year, and even though she was paid for the holidays, she would have rather had the holidays off altogether. Vicki says, "We've talked about how to arrange our schedules in such a way as to balance out the holidays a little bit better."

Vicki and Jill have had to adjust to one another's habits and preferences; one of them had to put a potential promotion aside because the other one wasn't interested in pursuing it. However, citing their high priority for working part-time and a clause in their contract that requires one to return to work full-time if the other leaves, neither plans to give up the arrangement any time soon.

MAKING IT WORK WHEN YOU

TELECOMMUTE

The success of a telecommuting or work-at-home arrangement depends as much on your personality as on the nature of the job. Perhaps more than any other flexible option, it requires commitment and willingness on the part of your boss. Here's what we found to be the essentials for making it work:

Avoid distractions. Plan to make day-care arrangements for the time you work at home if your children need adult supervision. Don't get into the habit of mixing household chores with working at home. Throwing in a load of laundry can easily turn into folding, ironing, and putting clothes away.

Make sure you have the tools of the trade at home. Having the equipment you need to do the job is essential. At a minimum, it will be a telephone. But you may also need a computer, modem, and fax machine. Some employers loan "retired" equipment but will usually not purchase equipment for at-home workers. It is common, however, for an employer to pay for the cost of installing an extra phone line in an employee's home so that one line is kept clear for office use.

Build a trust relationship with your boss. Your boss must believe you're productive even if he or she can't see you working. That will be easiest to prove if you consistently deliver the same quality product your boss is used to getting.

Put a communication plan in place. Keep in touch with your boss and co-workers by establishing a regular time to check in with them, and let them know when and where you can be reached.

Be accessible to your boss and co-workers. Plan your schedule around regular staff meetings. Keep informed of other important meetings and work obligations so that you can arrange to be available to attend them whenever possible.

Trust and Commitment Make It Work

Loren Wright, a systems software analyst and part of a U S WEST group located in Bellevue, Washington, has found a creative way to handle family and business responsibilities, cut down on his 43-mile, one-way commute, and still have time for volunteer work and his passion for remote control airplanes.

Loren's work arrangement combines telecommuting with a compressed workweek schedule and is designed to complement his wife's part-time schedule as a nurse. He works at home every Monday from 4:30 a.m. until about 2:30 p.m. when his elementary school-age children get home. Then he works 10-hour days at his office Tuesdays, Wednesdays, and Thursdays. He has Fridays off.

Loren's schedule is possible because his manager made it known that she is open to a variety of flexible schedules including flextime and telecommuting. Loren says the schedule makes sense from a business perspective because, "For the type of work I do, I'm not tied to a particular location." He further explains, "I'm on call seven days a week, 24 hours a day to troubleshoot problems. When an emergency call comes in at 2:00 a.m., I can be 'at work' instantly and avoid an hour-long trip to the office."

Loren feels his arrangement works because his manager, Gerri Tyler, trusts him and the other eleven people in his group who also telecommute to varying degrees. To get around the pitfalls of dealing with the schedules of thirteen people, Gerri says, "We have a staff meeting every Thursday morning—the one time that everyone is expected to be in the office. If someone can't make it, which happens occasionally, they attend by phone."

When asked what makes a telecommuting arrangement work, Gerri says, "Telecommuters need to be self-motivated and really like what they do so they don't get sidetracked while they work at home." And Loren adds, "It takes a manager who has to be able to let go and an employee who has to produce results."

WHAT TO DO IF IT'S NOT WORKING

Flexible work options are rarely problem free. Most people we've talked to felt that, over all, managers and co-workers were supportive of their flexible schedules. However, it's not uncommon to hear accounts of jealous co-workers, reassigned office space, snide remarks, and sloweddown career advancement.

Lynn Bolles, a research scientist, told us that when she started working part-time after several years of working full-time for the same company, she was moved with no warning at all from her windowed office to a small interior cubicle. She also lost her parking space. "Despite my anger, I knew I couldn't win this battle without some heavy artillery," she told us. "It took me eighteen months, but I won my office back after I had time to chalk up some major successes as a part-timer. I was never reassigned a parking space, but shortly after I got my office back, I negotiated a parking subsidy as part of my benefits package."

Mary Burgess, a technical editor, was hired for a part-time job as a new employee but was constantly harangued by a boss who wanted her to work more hours. She was also snubbed by a co-worker who was jealous that Mary had the "luxury" of working part-time.

"After a year of many gentle and not-so-gentle reminders of the hours and salary I committed to when I was hired, I quit," says Mary. "I believed that the people I worked with would never be able to make the adjustment to having a part-time professional in the office."

Whether you're working part-time or using your own brand of a flexible schedule, the following are the most common problems you're likely to encounter. Suggestions follow for getting positive results. Choose the solutions that speak best to your situation.

Getting Around the Common Stumbling Blocks

Problem: Co-workers are jealous of or seem annoyed by your schedule.

Solution: If you're working part-time, remind co-workers that you may be working less, but you're earning less money and have fewer benefits, too. If you're using a flexible full-time schedule, remind them you're working the same number of hours they are, just not at the same time.

Solution: Keep work and personal life separate. Don't brag about all the great things you do on your days off.

Solution: Avoid taking long lunches and using work time to tend to personal matters.

Problem: You're routinely working more hours than you're being compensated for.

Solution: Analyze your situation to decide how to adjust your work load. This may involve keeping a log of your activities to identify what duties could be reassigned to others or to make the case for hiring someone to help you.

Solution: If you're taking on too many assignments, set limits on your time and stick by them. Let your co-workers and boss know you are not available for more than the agreed-upon hours per week.

Solution: Renegotiate your agreement to work more hours, with salary and benefits increased accordingly.

Solution: Request an hourly rate instead of a salary. This will provide your supervisor with an extra incentive to keep your hours where they should be if she's working within a budget.

Solution: Consider a job-share partner.

Problem: You're not being taken seriously by your colleagues.

Solution: Conduct yourself in a professional manner. Dress the part, be on time, and be prepared for meetings and appointments. Be confident about your ability to get the job done.

Solution: Be aggressive about getting "plum" assignments. Talk to your boss directly about the expectations you have for yourself and the kind of work you want to do. If projects tend to be large, suggest taking responsibility for those parts that can best use your knowledge and skills.

Solution: Send a strong message about your commitment to co-workers by making time for special activities. Taking on the supervision of student interns or coordinating a presentation for the board of directors, for example, shows your interest in being a team player.

Solution: Stay visible to colleagues by making presentations to outside groups, serving on the board of directors of a professional association, getting articles published in your field, and pursuing other professional achievements outside of work.

Problem: Meetings are scheduled for times you don't work or for times when you're working at home.

Solution: Attend a meeting scheduled for a time when you're not supposed to be at work, and then ask the person responsible for scheduling to accommodate your schedule the next time.

Solution: If you can't physically attend a meeting, ask that you be included by speaker phone.

Solution: Be flexible and switch workdays or hours if necessary to attend the most important meetings. You're the best judge of when it's worth the effort.

Solution: Since managers usually call meetings, let their secretaries know your hours so they can keep them in mind when they're doing the scheduling.

Solution: As soon as you hear that a meeting is being arranged, focus on the positive, not the negative, by suggesting the times you are available to meet.

Solution: Give everyone as much notice as possible whenever your schedule changes.

Problem: Your career advancement has come to a screeching halt.

Solution: If a career path was not spelled out when you negotiated or accepted your job, ask to address the issue at your next annual review, or suggest a meeting to discuss the issue.

Solution: Keep your skills up-to-date by requesting to be included in training programs or by seeking classes on your own.

Solution: Occasionally accept extra work to help out a co-worker or to raise your profile, even if it means putting in more time for a while.

Solution: Ask to supervise staff and manage projects, even on a small scale, to show your interest in taking on more responsibility.

Solution: Be available for business travel whenever possible. Attending company meetings, representing your organization at conferences or meetings, and working for out-of-town clients show a high level of commitment to your job.

Once you start a new work arrangement, you may encounter bumps along the way, but don't let these temporary setbacks discourage you. Unless you find yourself in an extreme situation where you really believe your job will never work to your advantage, think creatively and stick with your plan to work the kinks out.

TO SUM IT UP

✔ Believe in yourself and in your new work arrangement.

✔ Be flexible.

✔ Engage reliable, dependent care.

✔ Plan short- and long-term goals for yourself so that your career stays on track.

✔ Let co-workers know if your schedule changes.

✔ Find time to do a little socializing with colleagues at work.

✔ Be candid with your boss about your expectations for the job.

✔ Set limits on your availability when you're not working.

✔ Tell colleagues how you want to be represented to the public.

✔ Take advantage of office technologies to maximize efficiency.

✔ Keep work and personal life separate.

✔ Go the extra mile once in a while to get the job done.

PART 4

More Alternatives

CHAPTER 9

FINDING A NEW FLEXIBLE JOB

Find a job that
is fit for you,
rather than one
you think you
might be able to
fit into.

— *Ronald L. Krannich*

There's no question that anyone looking for a job today faces a challenge. Add to that a job with a flexible schedule and you may feel you're biting off more than you can chew. But armed with the advice that follows, a healthy dose of creative thinking, and a little good luck, you *can* find the job of your dreams.

In this chapter, we'll take a look at the major trends shaping today's job market and highlight the industries we think hold the greatest promise for creating new flexible jobs. We offer some pointers for maximizing your job search and we'll clue you in on some of the tried and tested strategies (such as applying for a full-time job when you want to work part-time) that other job hunters have used to find the "perfect" job.

Note: If you need a refresher course on the ins and outs of a job search, there are a lot of good resources available, many of which are mentioned in Appendix C: Future Readings.

TUNING INTO THE TRENDS

The "reengineering" of corporate America (one of today's euphemisms for laying off workers), the rise in small business, and the rapid decline of some of the country's biggest industries such as defense and manufacturing, has, in a few short years, turned the economy and the job outlook upside down. Another catalyst of change—advancing technology—is transforming the nature of jobs overnight, opening up new work opportunities for people who live in remote areas of the country, while making other traditional jobs obsolete.

In fact, since 1979, Fortune 500 companies have cut 4.4 million jobs from their ranks. And there's no end in sight. You can hardly pick up the morning paper or turn on the evening news without hearing about another layoff. It's happening all over—in government agencies, at manufacturing plants, and at the headquarters of major corporations. And it's affecting tens of thousands of people.

Fortunately, the picture isn't entirely bleak, thanks in large measure to small business. In its July 1993 issue, *Working Woman* magazine reported that virtually all new jobs in the United States between 1988 and 1992 were created by small business, with firms of nineteen or fewer employees responsible for 78 percent of that increase.[1]

That's good news—especially if you're looking for a job with flexibility. Many start-up companies, as well as associations, hospitals, nonprofit organizations, private schools, colleges, and consulting groups, are eager to draw top talent, but they aren't always in the position to compete with the salary and benefits offered by large employers. What they can and do offer, though, is flexible schedules. And this has given them a real edge in attracting and keeping top talent.

Gay Torrance is one example. President of Torrance and Associates, a small public relations firm that employs eight people, she told *Inc.* magazine that offering flexibility to her employees is how she keeps them on staff. She said, "I've been able to keep the people I have because they have families, children, and spouses, and I'm flexible about that. I allow them to have a life. In return, they work extra when they have to."[2]

The Fastest-Growing Industries

Hardly an American industry escaped the 1991 recession unscathed. Coming on the heels of deregulation and the merger and acquisition mania of the 80s, few had the resources to weather the rough economic climate of the past several years without long-term effects. However, for many industries, the outlook is brightening as the economy starts to bounce back.

More good news is that a growing global economy marked by international competition and the continued explosion of computers and information services are jump-starting the economy and generating new jobs in numerous industries. Service-related industries are taking the lead here in creating jobs. Nearly 23 million of the 24.6 million new jobs anticipated by the year 2005 will be in the service sector.[3]

Keeping in mind our research, our experience with the types of job-opening announcements employers send to the Association of Part-Time Professionals (APTP), and the current trends in business, including the boom of the health industry, the "graying of America," the lowering of trade barriers, the ever-growing opportunities for independent consultants and temporary workers, and the sophistication of computer technology found at home and at work, we've picked ten growth industries we think hold the greatest promise for flexible jobs through the 90s. They are: advertising and public relations, business services, computers and electronics, education and training, financial services, health care, publishing, social and human services, telecommunications, and travel.

Jobs for Flexibility Seekers

If you're in tune with the trends, your skills are up-to-date, and you have an open mind about applying your interests and skills to jobs in more than one industry, you can find flexibility in a number of places.

For instance, if you're a teacher looking for a bigger paycheck and a more flexible schedule, you might very well create a career for yourself in the private or public sector as a trainer, many of whom are hired as independent contractors. And nurses, therapists, doctors, and numerous others in the medical field will have lots of work opportunities in the future beyond the doctor's office and the hospital. Long-term-care facilities and residential centers for the elderly and on-site corporate medical centers established to contain insurance costs are just two examples of new places where jobs can be found.

And, as has always been the case, the name of the game for flexibility is still supply and demand. If your skills and expertise are sought after—accountants, paralegals, word processors, home-care aides, nurses, pharmacists, and translators immediately come to mind—you can often name your schedule.

This goes double if you're in the computer field. Some of the hottest job opportunities will go to computer operators, service technicians, software engineers, systems analysts, and data-base managers, which are among the fastest-growing occupations in the economy and are projected to climb by more than 70 percent by the year 2000.[4]

As we head toward the 21st century, the stage is set for the wide acceptance of flexibility in the workplace. Though it's not yet entrenched the way we predict it'll be at the turn of the century, there are plenty of opportunities now. The best chance you have for finding a flexible job is to sharpen your skills so that you keep up with the competition and seek out jobs in industries that are on their way up. If you follow this advice, along with our job-seeking tips in the next part of the chapter, you'll be in an ideal position for getting the job offer you want.

ADVICE FOR STARTING YOUR JOB SEARCH

One of the most frequently asked questions we get at APTP is "What is the best way to find a flexible job?" Most people are surprised when we tell them that the "secret" is in applying the same basics of any good job search: getting the word out to everyone you know, researching companies in your field to find out who's hiring, getting your resume in shape, and following up every job lead in sight.

Job hunting is a job in itself. Here are some pointers to get the best results from your efforts:

Plan your strategy. Before you start poring over the classifieds, flooding the market with your resume, or scheduling interviews, map out a plan of attack. It will help you set realistic goals for the type of job to pursue and keep you from getting sidetracked along the way. If you're switching gears to find a job that eases the stress in your life or demands less of your time, consider transferring your skills to a different industry or pursuing a new field of interest.

Know what you want. Draw on your past experience and personal interests, and spend time at the library researching the job market to pinpoint the types of employers you'd like to work for. Since most occupations can be pursued in the public and private sectors as well as in nonprofits and associations, be sure to cover all your bases.

To avoid the risk of narrowing your focus too much, especially when you're looking for a job with flexibility, consider how your skills can be applied to a variety of jobs. For instance, a social worker looking for a new setting may find an interesting career path with a corporate employee assistance program or with private firms providing these services to the business community.

Know what you can afford. Looking for a job goes hand in hand with deciding on the life-style you want. If you're looking for a job with a flexible schedule, especially one that's part-time, you may have a better chance of finding one in the public sector, in the nonprofit community, or with a small business than in the corporate world. Most likely the salary won't be what you'd find at a Fortune 500 company, but if more time with your family is what you're after, the trade-off may be worth it.

Polish your resume. Your resume alone won't get you a job, but you'll never get one without it either. An essential ingredient of any job search, it's often the first impression you'll make with an employer you approach for a job. If you've used a flexible schedule or had a part-time job in the past, our advice is not to mention it in your resume unless it's advantageous to the position you're applying for. It's better to grab the attention of a potential interviewer with your credentials first, and bring up your interest in a flexible schedule later.

Get help. If you find the whole job-search process daunting, look for some outside help. There are plenty of good books on the market to help you develop a sound job-search plan, write an effective resume, or fine-tune your interviewing skills. Career counselors, support groups, community agencies, and outplacement firms can help with career and job counseling, resume preparation, job-search strategies, and interviewing techniques. (*A word of caution*: Be wary of job-search services that come with a high price tag—they usually aren't worth it. And similar, if not better, services are often available through a state or county employment center.)

Be prepared to switch gears. If you're not getting the results you want, you may have to readjust your strategy. If your ideal job doesn't come along right away, consider taking an interim position, such as a temporary job, until you can find the job you really want. And don't forget that many people have found a new career and greater job satisfaction by changing industries, pursuing a new line of work, and even relocating to a different city with a different job market.

Be tenacious. There's no substitute for persistence. Searching for the right job can be a tiring and frustrating task, but it's important to stick with it. Doing something to advance your job search every day will help you keep your spirits up and sustain your momentum until you achieve your goal.

GETTING YOUR FOOT IN THE DOOR

When you're hunting for a job—part-time or full-time—use every resource and contact at your disposal. Leave no stone unturned—you never know which job lead, friendly suggestion, or hunch is going to pay off.

Following the Traditional Routes

Thousands of people continue to find jobs through the "visible" market—classified ads, government announcements, and recruiting firms. And following up personal contacts and referrals—generally known as networking—is an indispensable strategy for every job seeker.

Classified Ads

The employment section of newspapers, newsletters, and magazines usually list jobs under the headings of "full-time" and "part-time." However, we've found that employers don't necessarily stick to these distinctions. Many who advertise part-time professional vacancies routinely list their openings under the full-time section to draw from the widest range of candidates.

While local and regional newspapers are probably your best bet, don't overlook major business periodicals such as the *Wall Street Journal* or the *National Business Employment Weekly,* both of which publish a help-wanted section with jobs listings from around the country. And trade journals specific to your industry, such as the *Chronicle of Higher Education* if you're in academia, have the most targeted leads.

Government Job Announcements

All information about government job vacancies, including part-time opportunities, is a matter of public record and available through county, state, and federal employment offices. For specific information about a variety of flexible workplace initiatives available at all levels of government, check with the U.S. Office of Personnel Management (OPM) at the federal level and with personnel offices at the state and local levels.

One example of a program at the federal level is the OPM Connection. Designed to match federal employees who want to work part-time with federal agencies seeking to fill vacancies suitable for either part-time or job-share arrangements, the program is available in Boston, Chicago, Los Angeles, and Washington, D.C. Further expansion is on hold until interest in the program picks up.

Employment Agencies and Professional Recruiters

Most employment agencies and professional recruiters limit their services to people looking for full-time work. And they're known more for the high cost of their services than for consistent results. But a new, hybrid service that combines employment recruitment with career counseling for professionals, especially women who want to work part-time, began to appear in the late 1980s. Usually started by human resources specialists looking for flexible jobs themselves, they're springing up all over the country. The ones that have been around the longest are Part-Time Resources in Cos Cob, Connecticut; Professional Alternatives in Minnetonka, Minnesota; and Executive Options in Northbrook, Illinois (see Appendix B: Resources).

Networking

Long proclaimed by employment specialists, career counselors, and job seekers themselves as the number one way to land a job, networking is also one of the best strategies for finding a flexible job. Your network can connect you with unpublished job openings and put you in touch with people you may not otherwise have access to on your own. As Julie Cline, an association manager who's held three part-time jobs, put it, "It's been the key to finding every part-time job I've had."

As you set out to build your network, don't assume that you don't "know anybody." In fact, the people you see every day may turn out to be your most valuable source of contacts; they know you the best and are often the most eager to help you out. And you never know; the Little League coach or the sister of a neighbor may work for the very company that is at the top of your most desirable employers list.

Networking is the ultimate numbers game. Every person you talk to about your job search has the potential to pass your resume on to someone else. Your network can be as far-flung as you want to make it, but at a minimum should include your family, friends, neighbors, teachers, current and former employers, colleagues, co-workers, and acquaintances from community activities.

When you first meet someone new, don't try to hide the fact that you're looking for a job, even if you've been laid off. You'll get a lot further with people if they know exactly what you're looking for—information, advice, or referrals. (And remember, networking works best when it goes both ways. Some day you may be expected to return the favor by opening your Rolodex to someone who has been generous with referrals to you.)

Telling your immediate circle of family and friends that you're job hunting is only the first step in getting the word out. You should also dedicate time to cultivating new contacts. This may include joining or reactivating your membership in professional associations or contacting your college or university alumni or career development office. These offices usually operate a clearinghouse or job bank for students and alumni, and many provide access to computerized job-service networks and alumni directories.

Perhaps the most fertile ground for meeting new people in your field is to attend professional seminars and conferences, where prospecting for business and job leads seems high on everyone's agenda!

Another excellent way to widen your net of contacts is to volunteer. It's a great way to meet new people and it's the best way to get your foot in the door of an organization you really want to work for. And, if you're unemployed, volunteering can help you update your skills, add practical experience to your resume, and help you feel connected with the world of work during your job search.

Networking for a Job

&

"As soon as I realized I had to find another job, I started making phone calls, lots of phone calls," recalls Ingrid Peterson, a radiologist at one of the largest medical centers in Seattle, Washington. "I knew it wouldn't be easy finding a part-time job. The good jobs—those with job security and benefits—are almost never advertised in my field of medicine. Most of the good part-time jobs are found through word of mouth."

Ingrid found herself searching for a new job when her boss refused to consider a part-time arrangement following the birth of her second son. "I was adamant about working part-time," she remembers. "One of the reasons I chose radiology was because I felt the work was better suited to a part-time schedule than were other branches of medicine. I wanted time to participate in my kids' lives, not just show up now and then," she says. Looking for every advantage, Ingrid kicked her networking into high gear and was very up-front with everyone she talked to about her desire to work part-time. She recalls, "I knew I had to be candid to avoid getting sucked into taking a full-time job."

After four months of intensive networking, Ingrid found her new job through a colleague. "The timing couldn't have been better. The center was in an unusual phase of adding five new radiologists all at once so they had a little more leeway in how they filled the positions. It also didn't hurt that I had a contact on the inside."

Finding a New Niche

Judy McNamee had been an account executive with a large telecommunications firm for eight years when she approached her boss about a part-time schedule. When it became clear he wasn't going to warm up to the idea, she started to investigate her other options. She recalls, "I knew I couldn't do as well financially anywhere else so my preference was to look at other jobs that lent themselves to part-time work in the company."

Since she was the first person in sales to pursue a part-time schedule with the company, Judy knew she had to find the right job to make it work. After looking at other sales operations throughout the company, she hit on a good match in the technical sales division. Judy says, "A technical sales job fit the bill because I'd have less face-to-face contact with the customer, no overall account responsibility, and discrete projects to work on."

Judy's boss agreed she was on the right track and planned to make the pitch on her behalf to the manager of the technical division. But Judy insisted on making the presentation herself. She explains, "I wanted to represent myself so that I could personally show my commitment to making the job work." She also went prepared to sell her idea from a business perspective. "I took a one-page proposal that outlined the responsibilities I was willing to take on and a cost-benefit analysis to show the financial benefit to them and to me." Judy made a terrific impression. Convinced that Judy knew what she was getting into and seeing the potential in getting an employee with a good track record, the manager took Judy's proposal up the executive chain to seek approval for the request. Looking back, Judy says, "It took six months and several levels of approval, but the wait was worth it. I'm in a great job that has long-term potential. I'm paid well for the work I do and I've hung on to to my full benefits package, which was very high on my list of priorities."

TOUGH TIMES CALL FOR UNUSUAL MEASURES

Today's tight job market has forced many job seekers to become more creative in their search for the right combination of job and work schedule. If you're seeking permanent part-time employment, you know that ferreting out job opportunities is a real challenge. Here are some novel approaches others have used to find a flexible job.

Creating a New Opportunity with Your Current Employer

Just because your boss turns down your request for a flexible schedule, don't assume all other doors in your organization are closed to you. A manager with a different attitude in another department or division may see the benefit of getting an experienced employee to join his or her team on a part-time basis. And if your goal is to work part-time, you're almost always better off staying with your employer when it comes to salary and benefits.

Applying for a Full-Time Job When You Only Want to Work Part-Time

In addition to using the traditional job-search strategies, some people looking for jobs are taking a more innovative approach: They're responding to full-time job vacancies, hoping to sell a prospective employer on a part-time arrangement.

This might be a good strategy for you, especially if you have a highly sought after skill or expertise. Whether you suggest part-time or job sharing will depend on the type of job, the kind of schedule you want, your own career goals, and if you have knowledge about the employer's attitude about flexible work arrangements.

There are two ways to go about it. You can raise the issue in the cover letter accompanying your resume, or you can broach the subject during the interview. Either way involves some risks. If you mention it in your cover letter, you stand the chance of having your resume tossed into the wastebasket before it gets into the hands of the person conducting the interview. Likewise, waiting to raise your interest in working part-time until your first or second interview may anger the employer if he thinks you're not serious about wanting the job he is trying to fill.

Creating New Job Leads
───────────────── ❧ ─────────────────

Betsy Walton works three days a week as a marketing specialist for a trade association in Virginia. She landed the job by applying for a full-time position advertised in the Sunday employment supplement of her local newspaper.

Before that, a year-long stint at temping had been interesting and fun. "Temping was a great way to have the flexibility I needed, but I was getting tired of starting and quitting jobs," she said. "After some soul-searching, I realized I wanted something more permanent— but only part-time."

Betsy had always worked in the nonprofit arena. Starting off on the financial side, she like many others, had learned to wear a variety of hats, adding new areas of expertise to her resume over time. Willing to consider a wide range of jobs, Betsy turned to canvassing the full-time work section of the newspaper for jobs she found interesting and felt she was qualified for.

Betsy decided she had nothing to lose by mentioning her interest in part-time work in her cover letter. "I'm a firm believer in being upfront about my intentions to work part-time," says Betsy. "In my cover letter I say: 'I'm available on a part-time basis. Would you be willing to consider it?'" This sends a clear message to the employer and puts him in the driver's seat if he wants to follow up.

Betsy's approach worked. As it turned out, the manager who hired Betsy had never considered hiring a part-timer until Betsy raised the possibility. The job had been redefined since they placed the ad, and hiring Betsy to fill the marketing slot on a part-time basis proved to be an unexpected, but welcome, cost-saving measure.

Not every full-time job lends itself to a part-time schedule. And not every employer will be as receptive to the idea as Betsy's employer was. As a matter of fact most employers who list full-time positions are already convinced the job can only be done on a full-time basis. If you find that's the case, maybe Camilla Lopez's story, which follows, will be helpful.

The Job-Share Approach

Camilla Lopez felt her best chance for being hired for the program development position at the Educational Resource Institute in Denver was to find someone to share the job with. "The position required fluency in Spanish and at least five years of extensive experience developing an elementary school curriculum. The language was certainly no problem, but since I had just received my degree in education, I was short on practical experience," explains Camilla. "I desperately wanted the job but only on a part-time basis."

Camilla had come through the first interview with flying colors and felt certain that she would be called in for a second one. "But I was also left with the distinct impression that proposing a part-time schedule would instantly take me out of the running," she comments. "It was pretty clear the demands of the job required a full-time person."

A neighborhood gathering put Camilla in touch with Sandy Dirksen. One thing led to another and it wasn't long before Camilla learned Sandy was an education specialist who also happened to be looking for a part-time job. "It just clicked," Camilla said, "and it didn't take us long to realize that together we could present an impressive package of experience to the institute."

Camilla's first interview gave her a foot in the door. As a follow-up she sent a copy of Sandy's resume and a letter outlining how their combined professional experience would benefit the organization. It worked. After two more sets of interviews, they were hired.

"Selling them on a job-share arrangement turned out to be easier than we thought. The combination of our skills clinched it for us because together we brought more to the job than any other single candidate. It's clearly a win-win situation for all of us," Camilla says.

You may have gotten your foot in the door with a striking cover letter and resume like Camilla and Betsy, or with a few well-placed words from a colleague like Ingrid, earlier in this chapter. But that's only half the battle. Now it's time for you and your potential employer to size each other up and close the deal.

INTERVIEWING FOR A FLEXIBLE JOB

When you're interviewing for a job, it's as important for you to find out about the employer as it is for the employer to find out about you. This especially holds true when you're in the running for a flexible full- or part-time job. Besides making a good impression, getting to the bottom of the employer's expectations for you and the job should be a top priority. For example, if a job with heavy responsibilities is advertised for 30 hours a week without benefits, is the employer trying to shore up the budget or does she really need someone only three or four days a week? The best way to find out is by asking the right questions during the interview.

From the interviewer's perspective, she's the one who's supposed to be quizzing you, but more than likely you'll be given an opportunity to ask some questions of your own. If you know you'll be seeing more than one person, it may be best to save some of your questions for future interviews. But be sure you get the answers to your most pressing questions from the person you'd be reporting to. We've drawn up a list of questions you should get answered, but don't be limited by these. Think of others that pertain specifically to the kind of work you do and the responsibilities of the job.

Interview Questions

Here's our set of questions to ask when you're interviewing for a flexible job:

- Does the organization have flexible work policies in place, or are flexible schedules offered on a case-by-case basis?

- What will my opportunities be for career advancement?
- How many other people in the organization use flexible schedules?
- How will the staff feel about a newcomer using a flexible schedule?
- Is this a permanent position?

Add these questions to the list if you're interviewing for a part-time job:

- Is this a new position? If so, whose idea was it to create a part-time position? And why? If it's not a new position, how many hours a week did the last person work? Was he or she successful in meeting the goals of the job?
- Are there other part-timers on staff? If so, in what positions?
- In the event of a staff cutback, are part-timers the first to go?
- What benefits do you offer to part-time employees?
- If I work extra hours, will I be compensated with extra pay or comp time?
- Is it possible to make a transition from a part-time to a full-time job in the future?

CLOSING THE DEAL

After you've navigated the job-search process and weathered the interview, your first reaction to a job offer may be a huge sigh of relief. But don't let your guard down yet. You still have the most important task ahead—negotiating the terms of the job.

If you're negotiating a flexible full-time job, your main concern will be the schedule you commit to. While agreeing on a schedule is just as important in a part-time job, negotiating a salary and benefits package should also command a good deal of your attention.

Below, we've highlighted the main points to keep in mind when you're negotiating a flexible job. However, we also suggest you refer back to chapter 7 for a more thorough discussion on this topic. Even though that chapter addresses someone who's redesigning his or her current job, you'll find much of the advice appropriate for your situation, too.

Points to Keep in Mind During
Your Negotiation

When negotiating your schedule:

- Don't take on more work than you think you can handle on the proposed schedule.
- If you want to work a different schedule than the one that's being offered (i.e., you want to work three full days and the employer wants you to be available for five short days), suggest a trial period so that you can show that the schedule you want can work. Failing that, suggest a compromise.
- If you don't plan to be in the office every day because you're working part-time or telecommuting, agree on your availability for meetings that are scheduled for the times you're not on site. You may want to suggest that you attend important meetings by conference call.
- Don't be too quick to say you're always available, or you may find yourself working many more hours than you're being paid for.
- If travel is involved, decide on how you'll handle your schedule during the time you're away.

When negotiating a salary and benefits package:

- Bargain for the best deal you can get. Remember, future raises will be linked to the money you agree on up-front and your benefits may never change.
- Know how much money you want to earn and what kind of benefits you need to get to make the job worthwhile to you.
- If health insurance is out of the question, and you don't have coverage through a spouse, negotiate more money so you can afford to purchase it on your own.
- Don't overlook the importance of paid leaves. You stand to lose a lot of income if you're not paid for vacation, sick, and holiday leave.
- Agree on comp time or additional pay for extra hours worked.
- You may want to negotiate an hourly rate instead of a salary if you suspect the number of hours you work will fluctuate.

TO SUM IT UP

✔ Stay informed of the industries with the most job opportunities. Growing industries always have room for well-trained workers.

✔ Keep an open mind about transferring your skills to occupations that are in the greatest demand.

✔ Small businesses are creating the vast majority of new jobs.

✔ Take the time to put together a quality resume.

✔ Build a network that's as wide as possible. The more people who know you're looking for a job the better off you'll be.

✔ Consider approaching employers for a flexible job even if they only advertise full-time positions.

✔ When interviewing for a flexible job, be sure you and the employer have the same expectations.

✔ Negotiate the schedule you want and the best salary and benefits package you can get.

CHAPTER 10

OTHER CAREER TRACKS: GOING OUT ON YOUR OWN AND TEMPING

Find out what

you like doing

best and get

someone to pay

you for doing it.

— Katherine

Whitehorn

Y ou may feel that your pursuit for
flexibility has eluded you, but don't despair. If getting the flexible schedule
you want seems impossible with your current employer, finding a new job
hasn't worked out, or you want to continue working but at your own pace,
you still have two other options to consider: self-employment and temping.
It may be easier than you think to support yourself by setting up shop at
home or signing on with a temp help company. If you have a skill that's in
demand and the temperament to work independently, you can earn a decent
income and find the flexibility you've been looking for.

Self-employment and temping have taken the workplace by storm. For
employers who have scaled back their staffs at an alarming pace, they offer
a guarantee of workers. For you, they can be the solution to working when,
where, and how you want to. And for all of us, they may be the future of the
American workplace.

We interviewed CEOs of temp help companies, numerous people who
have their own businesses, and several people making a living by combining contracting with temping. What follows are their insights along with
our own to give you an overview of the pros and cons of both options, a
comparison of the two, and advice for getting started. It's by no means the
whole story on either alternative. But it will help you decide at this point in
time whether being your own boss or working as a temp is better than
getting a permanent job with an employer.

If you're tempted to give one of these options a try, there are dozens of
good how-to books you can turn to for more detailed information. We've
suggested a few in Appendix C: Further Readings, but we particularly like
Working from Home by Paul and Sarah Edwards, and *The Temp Track* by
Peggy O'Connell Justice. Both books cover almost all you need to know
before trying your hand at either one.

THERE'S NEVER BEEN A BETTER
TIME TO BE AN INDEPENDENT

Whether you consider yourself home-based, an independent contractor, an entrepreneur, a freelancer, or a consultant, it all boils down to the same thing: You're hanging out your own shingle to turn your job skills into a profitable business. You may be striking out on your own because you've lost your job unexpectedly, you've been denied a flexible work schedule, or you've always had a secret desire to be your own boss. Whatever your reason, you're in good company. The number of self-employed Americans has doubled in the last decade, bringing the total close to 30 million people!

One of these is Katherine Murphy, a mid-level marketing manager who was in the midst of redesigning her full-time position (she was typically working 50 to 60 hours a week) to part-time when she fell victim to a corporate restructuring. Out of work, she started the search for a new job.

"My goal was to find an interesting, challenging professional position that would provide some degree of flexibility. What I really wanted was to work part-time, four days a week," Katherine recalls. But her search to find the right part-time job was taking longer than she anticipated. She decided she had two choices: Look for a "reasonable" (40 hours per week) full-time job, or start a consulting business. Katherine opted for the independent consulting route because it held the greatest promise for the flexibility she was looking for. "Also," she says, "I was growing short on patience and resources."

Her strategy paid off. Katherine quickly landed a two-month, four-day-a-week stint with a small start-up company. She was again contributing to the coffers at home and, impressed with her work, Katherine's first client offered her a permanent part-time job at the end of the contract, which she accepted.

Barbara Hardman, a specialist in computer security, also went out on her own, but for different reasons and with different results. Barbara's part-time position at Harvey's Casino in Reno, Nevada, was the springboard for starting her consulting business. Her flexible three-day-a-week schedule was working out fine until she and her husband adopted a second child. At about the same time, her work load increased and her boss was pressuring her to work full-time. All this happened during one particularly snowy winter.

"As roads became impassable and I found myself traveling 3 hours for 4 hours of work, I decided it was time to make some changes," she says. Since Barbara's boss didn't want to lose her expertise and she didn't want to give up her career, they settled on a consulting arrangement that kept her in the loop on an as-needed basis.

Growing Markets for Independents

A great boost for self-employment is coming from the business community itself, which is relying more than ever on corporate outsourcing (using independents as needed) to shore up massive staff cutbacks. Outside contractors are routinely engaged to replace entire departments—such as accounting, travel, and data processing—once staffed by permanent full-time employees. In fact, your first client may well be your last employer, happy to rehire you on a contractual basis.

Changing demographics have also given rise to the emergence of new small businesses across the country. More mothers out of the home and in the workplace, for example, has increased the need for child-care programs and services. This, in particular, helped to open up a business opportunity for Pamela Henderson.

A mother of three children, Pamela was convinced she wasn't the only parent who couldn't get her three kids everywhere they needed to go all the time. That frustration gave birth to her own transportation service for children.

Pamela sent fliers to 200 parents, polling their interest in her plan. Overwhelmed by 600 responses in three days, she knew she had hit on something promising. Shortly after, she started Kids Kab, a taxi service for children who need a lift to and from after-school activities while their parents are at work. In two years she expanded from three vans transporting children around a Detroit suburb to a business with twenty-eight locations in twelve states.[1]

More Technical Support Than Ever

The availability of inexpensive computers, printers, copiers, fax machines, and other office equipment in recent years has made it easier and less expensive to run a business from home or from a small rented space. It's a good bet you already own a computer and a calculator. And even if you don't, for a few thousand dollars you can probably set yourself up with the office technology you've grown accustomed to in the workplace.

WORKING ON YOUR OWN: IS IT FOR YOU?

What do you need to go out on your own? First, and most importantly, you need marketable skills you can parlay into enough cash to meet your needs.

A large measure of self-discipline is essential for seeing your assignments through from beginning to end. If you've been in the workplace for a while you know that the structure provided by a supervisor, a designated work space, and the almighty paycheck are powerful.

And, third, you need to be a risk-taker, especially if you're staking your savings on the success of your venture. It can be a feast or famine proposition, yet if you're emotionally—and financially—prepared for the ups and downs of working for yourself, it can be challenging, exciting, and rewarding.

Good Reasons to Consider Self-Employment

You set your schedule. One of best things about being self-employed is the freedom to set your own hours. This is especially true for the growing number of men and women who are trading in job stress for job satisfaction by taking their work home—permanently. Being in control of your own work schedule gives you the greatest flexibility for working when you're most productive—early in the morning, late at night, or anytime in between—freeing the rest of your time for other activities.

If young children are in the picture, being able to work around the school day or during evenings and weekends when your spouse is available to help out can significantly reduce your child-care expenses. Or you can decide not to work during the holidays or summer months, as Sandy Cogan, a training specialist in Atlanta, Georgia, does.

"I try to schedule most of my work from January to May and September to mid-November," she says. "With five children, it's easier to keep life running smoothly." Sandy could not always afford to be that choosy. Until she established a reputation with her clients, Sandy lost business when she wasn't available. Now clients use her during the months she is available and fill in with other trainers when necessary.

You have control over your career. If you like your job but never seem to have enough time to do the things you want to do or you're frustrated by rigid demands at work, you may find more opportunity and challenge by being in business for yourself.

Carol Wang, a computer software designer, left the work force when her son was born instead of taking her boss up on his offer of a flexible schedule with no benefits and no career advancement. "It was a tough choice to make, but it wasn't worth it to me to stay in a dead-end job," Carol recalls. "But at the same time, I was worried my skills would become obsolete if I stayed out of the work force for too long."

After six months, Carol's old boss called her with a consulting assignment. She agreed to do it but only if she could work part of the time at home. When Carol realized how easy it was to call the shots as a contractor, she saw new possibilities in going back to work—this time for herself. Satisfied with her new role as an entrepreneur, Carol set up a small firm in 1988 that now boasts six employees—all women with similar work skills and demands on the home front.

Beth Nielsen, a mortgage underwriter, went out on her own for a different reason. She recalls, "I was tired of the slow-moving wheels of the corporate world and found the constant reorganization unsettling. I was pigeonholed in my job with nowhere else to go in the company and felt my best option was to leave and try to make it on my own."

Consulting has given Beth the job satisfaction she was looking for as well as the unexpected benefit of making better money. Her good reputation as a contractor has also kept her profile high in the industry. "I can pick and choose the assignments I accept," she says, "and I've turned down more than one job offer."

There is the potential to earn better money. If you're in the fortunate position of having a highly sought after skill or specialty, you may be able to work less and earn more. We've heard this from doctors, lawyers, top-notch word processors, writers, and many others who have turned their expertise into well-paying work.

Susan Cavoto, an occupational therapist who specializes in pediatric care in Chicago, attributes her success to having thirteen years of experience in a field that has an extreme shortage of therapists. "I have my pick of assignments," she explains, "and I make in three days what most permanently employed therapists make in five."

You avoid office politics. Ray Hermann, a San Fransciso–based attorney who's an independent consultant, told us, "One reason I left the law firm setting was because I wanted to practice law, not politics." At best, office politics are annoying, and at their worst, they can get in the way of productivity. Ray has consistently found that, even when he works at client sites, he's unlikely to be bothered by office politicking since he's not vying for attention or promotions.

Pitfalls to Watch Out For

Mismanaging your time can cost you time and money. Once you're on your own, you'll wear every hat in the business, from president to janitor. In the course of a day, you may sign off on a contract with a new client, pay the electric bill, type your own correspondence, and take out the trash. You may be good at juggling a variety of tasks; it may even appeal to your sense of organization and save you money. But if you're not careful, doing everything yourself can cost you plenty. Spending too much time on the day-to-day details of running a business can easily eat into your profits if you don't devote enough time to doing the work you're paid to do.

Dina Lorry, a home-based word processor, found she was devoting the majority of her time to worrying about administrative details such as organizing her files and not giving enough time to her billable work. She says, "Once I started working for myself, I had to change my old work habits. I did my billable work first thing in the morning when I felt fresh and I saved all my phone calls, bookkeeping, and correspondence for late afternoon and early evening."

The early morning hours that suited Dina so well may be all wrong for you. Be prepared to experiment with your schedule until you find one that's right.

You might feel isolated. Working alone isn't for everyone. You may miss the office camaraderie and opportunities to share ideas and concerns about your work more than you realize. Chatting over a cup of coffee or sharing a joke with a friend during a light moment is a good break from work and keeps the day moving.

If working at home will give you few opportunities to meet with colleagues or clients on a regular basis, make an effort to attend professional meetings and work at client sites occasionally to break the monotony.

When Morgan Harris left her employer to start an interior design business out of her home, she decided to join a professional association and a women's business organization. She recalls, "I was afraid I'd get into a rut by being at home so much. The groups I joined led to some great new business contacts and gave me a chance to get out and attend several meetings and social outings each month."

You can get sidetracked. Distractions are a common complaint from people who work at home. If you're like most of us, you'll need to fend off a potential stream of distractions, be it children clamoring for attention, a retired spouse looking for company, or a friend wanting to visit. Engaging child care is a must if you have small children who need supervision. And if you think you can take on more of the household chores just because you're home all day, you're likely to end up with a clean house and no bank deposits for the week.

Neighbors, friends, and relatives may need a gentle reminder that you'd prefer not to be disturbed during the times you've set aside to work. This is what Ken Ballour found out when he started a computer repair business in his basement. "Just because I was home all day, my neighbors thought I had time to meet every repairman and delivery truck they expected to arrive while they were at work," Ken says. "I finally started saying no, explaining I was working, too. It wasn't easy, but it was the only way to avoid the distractions."

You may have to cope with financial insecurity. Unless you're comfortable with some degree of risk, you may find it difficult to live with the financial ups and downs of a small business. More than likely, you won't be able to count on a steady income until you've built up your business. Clients who are delinquent paying their bills or who pull their business away with little notice can leave you in the lurch. And don't overlook the time you take off when you're sick or on vacation. When you're the boss, you don't get paid for the days you don't work.

Buying your own insurance can be a financial burden, too. "With a sizable mortgage to pay and two small children, the first thing I did was get disability and life insurance policies when I went out on my own," explains Michael Slom, an independent sales representative. "I couldn't afford to be vulnerable financially."

Unless you're covered by a spouse for health insurance, paying for a policy as an independent can be a staggering expense. Add to that a self-employed pension plan, life and disability insurance, and malpractice insurance if your clients require it, and you could be looking at funding a couple thousand dollars of insurance policies out of your own pocket each month. It's a temptation to put these purchases off, but even if money is tight, adequate insurance, especially health insurance, is no place to cut corners. We've all heard stories of people who've lost their savings overnight because of serious illness or injury.

There may be interference with your family life. Working at home can cause major disruptions to your family life unless you've set aside your own work space. Pick a quiet place, preferably a spare bedroom or study. You may feel selfish, but your family needs to understand that your office is only for you and your work.

Wendy Miller, a contracts procurement specialist, insists on absolute privacy from her family when she works at home. She says, "My home office is in an isolated part of the house far away from the kitchen, the family room, and a thousand other distractions. When I'm working with the door closed, my family knows I'm not to be disturbed."

Note: The IRS requests that your office be used solely for business if you plan to write off part of your mortgage and other at-home business expenses on your tax return.

Self-Employment as a Permanent Solution to Flexibility
❧

When Barbara Miller went into business for herself, she finally found the job of a lifetime. "What happened to me has happened to a lot of women," says Barbara, owner of Allied Health Professionals, Ltd., in Chicago, Illinois. "After I had a baby, I went back to work full-time, gave it a shot, and decided it wasn't what I wanted to do. I wanted to continue working, but preferred a flexible schedule to have more time with my daughter. I proposed a part-time arrangement to my boss, but when that was flatly denied, I prepared myself to leave the job," she recalls.

Determined not to give up working, Barbara started to explore her options, including the possibility of a career change. While she was still with her employer as director of marketing and strategic planning at a large hospital in Chicago, Barbara devoted many of her weekends and evenings to making her next move. In the beginning she sought the advice of a career counselor who specializes in helping executives make the transition to new careers.

Like many of us, Barbara has a varied background. Bearing in mind her education and training in speech therapy, her marketing experience, and her knowledge and interest in the culinary arts, she considered a broad range of options—opening a restaurant or a gourmet shop, joining the marketing side of a consulting group, creating a part-time job as an administrator at another hospital, or starting a contract services agency for rehabilitation therapists. She chose the latter.

(continued on next page)

(continued from previous page)

"Starting an agency was the idea I kept coming back to because it made the best use of my education and experience and it let me work from home," Barbara recalls. Seeing the tremendous potential in tapping an underutilized labor force—young female therapists who had, like herself, left the work force because of rigid working conditions—and placing them in temporary assignments in hospitals and clinics faced with a shortage of therapists seemed like the perfect niche.

Since 1986, Barbara's business has grown from one therapist to more than 80. She clocks in about 40 hours a week in a home office, splitting the time between days, evenings, and weekends. Barbara is sold on having her own business and explains how it meets her priorities: "It's the first job I've had that I thought I could stay with forever. I'm working as hard as I did at the hospital, but I'm doing it at my own pace and for my own benefit. The flexibility of my schedule and the control I have over the growth of my business lets me devote plenty of time to my family while making a significant financial contribution to our household."

ADVICE FOR GETTING STARTED ON YOUR OWN

If you have a service to sell and the motivation to get a business up and running, you *can* make a go of working on your own. The independents we talked to offered the following points to consider before getting started:

- **Be realistic about how much money you need to make and how many hours a week you'll need to work to meet this goal.** Can you earn enough and still end up with the flexible schedule you were searching for in the first place?

- **Organize your schedule to make the most of your day.** Tackle billable work when you feel fresh and save administrative chores for the least productive part of the day.
- **Consider your personality, temperament, and work style.** Ask yourself these questions: Are you suited to working alone or for a variety of clients who may all have pressing needs at the same time? Are you a self-starter who doesn't need to be prodded to get your work done? Do you trust your own judgment and act decisively when you're in a leadership role? Are you prepared to do whatever it takes to get the job done?
- **To minimize distractions, lay down some ground rules for family and friends.** If you plan to work from home, set aside a room just for working.
- **Keep in mind that working at home is no substitute for daycare.** You'll need to make arrangements for children and elder dependents who need meals prepared and frequent supervision.
- **Set aside enough savings to see yourself through the first six months since your income may be minimal in the beginning.** Are you prepared to live with the consequences if you invest and lose your nest egg?
- **Explore all your options for purchasing health, life, and disability insurance.** While you'll find a number of private plans available for life and disability policies, you'll find slim pickings when it comes to health insurance. Assuming you're still on the job, don't overlook the possibility of extending the policy you have with your current employer. Although you'll have to pay the full premium, it's a good way to get an additional eighteen months coverage at a group rate. If that's not an option, consider joining a professional association that offers group rates on insurance to its members.

TEMPING: THE ULTIMATE ROUTE TO FLEXIBILITY

Probably the biggest advantage of temping is the flexibility it allows you. Whether you're working around job interviews or the scout troop meetings you lead, you can pick and choose assignments to create the work schedule that suits you best. As one temp put it: "Temping is the ultimate route to a flexible schedule. I work where and when I want to and have as many days off as I need when I want to go on vacation or when one of my kids is sick."

The temp industry today is casting a much wider net around the industries they help and the people they recruit to serve their clients. The stereotypes that come to mind when you think of temps—the file clerk, fill-in secretary, or receptionist; the student in search of extra income; and the retiree not quite ready to step out of the work force—still hold true today, but they don't stop there. For the first time, a wide range of professionals has flooded the ranks of temp help companies: chemists, doctors, nurses, lawyers, computer specialists, engineers, writers, and other skilled professionals.

What's in Temping for You?

Temping can put money in your pocket, relieve the pressures of the daily 9-to-5 routine, or ease you through a transition such as moving to a new city. The following survey sums up the reasons why so many people are turning to temping:

Additional income	80%
Flexible work time	77%
Improve skills	70%
Looking for full-time work	67%
Between full-time jobs	52%
Less stress	50%
New to area	30%

Source: Robert Half International, Inc., 1993.

WHY TEMPING IS TAKING OFF

According to the National Association of Temporary Services (NATS), there are 1.3 million people working as temporaries today; that's three times as many as ten years ago.[2] Twenty-five percent of them are professionals or highly skilled workers who out of choice or necessity are working in short-term, nonpermanent work arrangements.[3] The "downsizing" of corporate America is responsible for this unprecedented boom in the temporary industry. Employers have found it more convenient and less costly to use temps when the work load demands rather than to maintain a large work force.

Temporary help companies still place the greatest number of temps in assignments, but an increasing number of large employers are creating their own temp pools, or registries, to sidestep the costs of using an outside firm. Some hospitals and corporations recruit their own temporary workers and call on them as the need arises. These temp pools are generally made up of former employees and people answering want ads. Much of the work is for people skilled in clerical work, health care, bookkeeping, and data processing.

Joining an in-house temping pool or registry can relieve some of the negatives of temping. Once you have an "in," you're likely to be called on regularly, giving you the luxury of working for one client in familiar surroundings with people you may eventually consider co-workers. You may also be able to take advantage of company-paid continuing education that will help keep your skills up-to-date at no cost to you.

WHAT YOU CAN EXPECT FROM TEMPING

Temp work generally means earning money quickly. When you go out on a job, you're often paid the same week you work. If you have a business of your own, temping is an excellent way to add to your income while you're getting your business off the ground or when your client work has slowed down. It can also be a good supplement to unemployment if you've been laid off, but it's wise to check with your unemployment office before signing up with an agency. In some states you'll put your unemployment benefits in jeopardy if you turn down a permanent job offered to you through your temping experience, even if it's one you have no interest in.

Another plus of temping is the potential to increase your earning power. One word processor we spoke with, who has top skills in three software packages, told us, "Even though I only work 30 hours a week, I doubled the earnings I was making from my full-time job because my agency commands a very high rate for my services. And although the health insurance policy isn't quite as extensive as at my last job, I'm still ahead of the game."

Above all, if your skills are highly sought after, you stand to make even more money as a temp than what you earned as a full-timer.

Despite its good points, temping is a fickle business. You can be yanked from long-term assignments without notice and you may not be called for several weeks at a time, both of which can lead to a shaky financial picture.

Read on to see if temporary work assignments are a good fit for you.

The Pros of Temping

Temporary work is an attractive alternative to permanent employment because it provides:

- a flexible schedule by giving you control over when and where you work
- an immediate source of cash if you're between jobs, retired, moving to a new city, changing careers, or starting a business of your own
- a way to increase your earning power. If you have highly marketable skills, you may be able to earn in three or four days what you've been used to getting in a full-time job
- a path to permanent employment. Temping is a good way to get visibility in a company you'd like to work for on a permanent basis.
- continuity of work so you don't have a gap on your resume
- another source of business contacts and potential references if you're job hunting or trying to build a clientele

- opportunity to upgrade and update your skills at the temp help company's expense

The Cons of Temping

Temping has its drawbacks. Traditionally, they include:

- lack of financial security since you're never guaranteed work or a steady paycheck
- lack of health and other insurances, as well as no paid sick and vacation leave, unless you work full-time or nearly full-time with one temp help company and have clocked in the required number of hours
- being an outsider; if you're looking for office camaraderie, temping may not be the place to find it
- less free reign on how you handle assignments; you'll need to conform to each workplace you're sent to and do the work the way they want it done
- difficulty in making dependent care arrangements if you don't know your schedule from one day to the next

ADVICE FOR GETTING STARTED AS A TEMP

If you don't want to run your own business, and you want the security of knowing someone else will find you work and pay you on time, then you're a good candidate for temping. The temps we talked to offered the following advice for getting off to a good start:

- First, you must have the tools. The skills and expertise you have under your belt must be marketable at a rate of pay that fits your budget.
- Upgrade and update your skills to stay abreast of changes in your field so you can compete for the highest-paying assignments. For instance, knowing more than one software application in your business will also make you more marketable.

- Sign up with one or more reputable agencies. If you have a specialty, work with the most prestigious agencies that concentrate in your area of expertise.
- You'll get off to a faster start with a temp help company if you make a good first impression by being prepared for your interview with an updated resume. Emphasize the skills you've learned in past jobs and make clear the variety of work you're qualified to do.
- Sign on with corporate in-house temping pools or registries. Many large companies and hospitals have their own temporary pools made up of former employees and others who want to work on an as-needed basis.
- Be flexible in accepting assignments. You'll get the most work if you're willing to accept jobs in a variety of settings in several locations within a geographic area.
- Don't wait for the phone to ring. Call the agencies you're working with weekly to remind them of your skills and your interest in working with a variety of clients.

INDEPENDENT CONTRACTING
VERSUS TEMPING

Since temping has found its way into the professions, independent contracting and temps are sometimes interchangeable; many people who have their own businesses often temp to earn additional income.

Mary Phillips, a writer-editor who is an independent contractor, often fell back on temping while she got her business off the ground. "As my business grew, I accepted only the jobs that paid the best or that gave me the visibility I wanted with certain companies," she explains. "Combining temp work with my own clientele is an ideal way to stick to the schedule I want and to keep the amount of money I need coming in."

Indeed, some temp help companies are beginning to place independent contractors in assignments. The temp company gets a flat rate for the

Highlights: Independent Contracting versus Temping

Independent Contracting

You have the entrepreneurial vision to start and cultivate a business. You find great satisfaction in working for yourself and feel challenged by running a business.

It takes time to market your services, perform the work, bill the client, and receive payment.

You'll usually make more money without a middleman taking a percentage of your fee.

You can tailor your schedule to meet personal needs and work when you want.

You can choose to work at home.

You plan your own calendar in advance so you know when you'll have time for nonwork activities or when you'll need to line up dependent care.

You'll be funding your own retirement plan and health, life, disability, and malpractice insurance plans.

You can have all the time off you want for sick and vacation leave, but you won't earn money when you don't work.

You foot the bill if you need to keep professional licenses current, such as attorney's bar fees, or if you attend conferences and training courses in your field.

Temping

You're happy to have someone else find work for you.

You see the obligations of running a business as a series of headaches; you would just as soon leave work behind you when you finish up for the day.

You'll find a quick source of cash in temping; a third party pays you regularly.

You'll never have to chase a delinquent client to pay you since the temp help company assumes all the risk.

Even when you have a long-term, full-time assignment, you can probably arrange time off when you need it. However, when you do work, you're expected to work during the client's hours of operation.

Temping assignments don't normally give you the option of working at home.

If you must have benefits, temping may be the better alternative. Some temp help companies extend a benefits package, including health insurance and paid leave for vacation and sick days, to temps who consistently work full-time or near full-time. More than likely, you'll be on your own to fund a retirement account.

You'll be on your own for keeping professional fees current, but if you temp full-time or near full-time for the same temp help company, you may qualify for an annual continuing education subsidy. If you're a regular with a corporate temp pool or hospital registry, you may be invited to attend their in-house training. Chances are they won't charge you a fee for the class, but they won't pay you for that time either.

placement and the temp negotiates his or her own fee for the services provided. Mixing the two options can be lucrative, but you may find it disruptive to switch gears between working for your own clients and working for the clients of a temp help company.

If you're still undecided about working for yourself or signing up with a temp help company, consider the comparisons between the two in the box.

TO SUM IT UP

✔ Self-employment and temping give you control over your schedule because you can choose when and where to work.

✔ You're a good candidate for starting your own business if you're a self-starter and you have a marketable skill.

✔ You're a good candidate for temping if you're comfortable in new situations and you work well with little supervision.

✔ You can work fewer hours and make more money consulting or temping if your skills are in high demand.

✔ As an independent contractor, you'll pay for your own insurance plans, including health. You'll also be responsible for keeping up your professional licenses and paying for continuing education courses.

✔ Some temps are eligible for health insurance and a subsidy toward continuing education credits if they work full-time or nearly full-time for one temp help company.

APPENDIX A: KEY STATISTICS FROM REPORTS AND SURVEYS ON FLEXIBLE WORK OPTIONS

Note: See Appendix B for a complete listing of resources, including most of those referred to here.

Prevalence of Flexible Work Arrangements

1. A 1989 survey by the Conference Board of 521 of the nation's largest companies revealed that 90 percent of the companies offer part-time, 50 percent offer flextime, 36 percent offer compressed workweek, 22 percent offer job sharing, 7 percent offer telecommuting, and 9 percent offer phased retirement programs.

    Source: Kathleen E. Christensen, *Flexible Staffing and Scheduling in U.S. Corporations.* The Conference Board, New York, 1989.

2. A 1990 survey of 645 organizations nationwide, released by the Hudson Institute, an Indianapolis research group, and Towers Perrin, a New York benefits consulting group, showed that 50 percent offer flextime, 47 percent have part-time workers, 22 percent offer job sharing, 16 percent have compressed workweek, and 4 percent have a school-days workweek.

    Source: "Workforce 2000, Competing in a Seller's Market: Is Corporate America Prepared?" The Hudson Institute and Towers Perrin, July 1990.

3. A 1990 study by the International Foundation of Employee Benefit Plans that surveyed 463 employers representing a cross section of industries shows the number of companies currently offering flexible work arrangements and the number that will add such programs by the year 2000.

Work Schedule	% That Currently Offer	% That Will Add by 2000
Part-time	80	14
Job sharing	24	43
Compressed workweek	22	29
Flextime	52	34
Telecommuting	15	37
Seasonal hours/school work year	27	19

Source: Nontraditional Benefits for the Workforce of 2000. International Foundation of Employee Benefit Plans, August 1990.

4. Sixty-five percent of the 177 companies polled offer part-time employment, 58 percent offer flextime, 16 percent allow telecommuting; 22 percent have employees who work a compressed workweek, 23 percent have job sharing, and 7 percent have a phased retirement program available to employees.

   Source: Work-Family Roundtable: Flexibility. The Conference Board, December 1991.

5. In a 1993 survey of 1,034 major U.S. employers, respondents stated that flexible scheduling arrangements are becoming increasingly popular in their organizations: 73 percent of the employers offer flextime, 67 percent offer part-time, 30 percent have job sharing, 21 percent offer compressed workweeks, and 16 percent allow work at home.

   Source: Work and Family Benefits Provided by Major U.S. Employers in 1993. Hewitt Associates, 1993.

Advantages of Flexible Work Arrangements

1. Ninety percent of the 153 participants responding to a Conference Board survey in 1991 stated that "response to employee request" was the primary reason for implementing flexibility. Other motivating factors included support of corporate image (71 percent), part of work/family initiative (64 percent), recruiting advantage (61

percent), support of work force diversity efforts (58 percent), increased productivity (56 percent), and preventing turnover (56 percent).

Source: Work-Family Roundtable: Flexibility. The Conference Board, December 1991.

2. Sixty-eight percent of employers interviewed by Catalyst in 1989 reported that the retention of employees is the most significant advantage of flexible work arrangements. Other advantages included a positive impact on recruitment (58 percent), higher productivity (65 percent), and improved morale (62 percent).

Source: Flexible Work Arrangements: Establishing Options for Managers and Professionals. Catalyst, 1989.

Related Topics

1. A recent survey of 902 women graduates of Harvard's Business School, Law School, and Medical School revealed that 85 percent consider a part-time schedule detrimental to a woman's career, 53 percent of the 594 mothers have changed jobs to accommodate family responsibilities, 39 percent believed that having children slowed their careers, and 85 percent responded that they have been able to combine family and career successfully.

Source: Deborah J. Swiss and Judith P. Walker, *Women and the Work/Family Dilemma: How Today's Professional Women Are Finding Solutions.* John Wiley & Sons, 1993.

2. The results of a six-month Bell Atlantic telecommuting pilot program in 1991 of fifty management employees showed that 27 percent improved their performance on the job and 73 percent maintained their same level of performance. The managers in this trial projected an annual savings of $15,000 in reduced gas consumption, public transportaion costs, and parking fees.

Source: General Telecommuting Guidelines. Bell Atlantic, 1992.

3. An analysis of corporate work-family programs at Johnson & Johnson in 1992 revealed 33 percent of the employees used the flexible work schedules program. Comparing the study to a similar one conducted in 1990, employees felt that when their immediate

supervisors' attitudes toward flexible work arrangements were more positive, workers were less likely to think they paid a price for using them.

Source: An Evaluation of Johnson & Johnson's Work-Family Initiative. Families and Work Institute, 1993.

Appendix B: Resources

American Association of Retired Persons (AARP)
1909 K Street, NW
Washington, D.C. 20049
(202) 662-4074
A nonprofit membership organization with nearly 4,000 chapters nationwide, it provides a variety of programs and services for persons 50 and older.

American Woman's Economic Development Corporation (AWED)
1250 24th Street, NW
Washington, D.C. 20037
(202) 857-0091
Provides training, counseling, and technical assistance to women who own or would like to start their own business.

Association of Part-Time Professionals (APTP)
7700 Leesburg Pike, Suite 216
Falls Church, VA 22043
(703) 734-7975
A national nonprofit membership organization that provides information and resources on flexible work arrangements to individuals and employers.

The Bureau of National Affairs, Inc. (BNA)
1231 25th Street, NW
Washington, D.C. 20037
(202) 452-4200
A private publisher specializing in public policy issues in the areas of employee relations, law, taxation, and work and family.

Catalyst
250 Park Avenue South, 5th Floor
New York, NY 10003-1459
(212) 777-8900
A national nonprofit organization that works with business to effect change for women through research, advisory services, and communication.

Clearing House on Work and Family
Women's Bureau
U.S. Department of Labor
200 Constitution Avenue, NW
Washington, D.C. 20210
(202) 523-4486
Provides information and research on work and family issues.

Conference Board, Inc.
Work and Family Information Center
845 Third Avenue
New York, NY 10022
(212) 759-0900
Provides information on work and family issues to business.

Executive Options, Ltd.
910 Skokie Blvd., Suite 210
Northbrook, IL 60062
(708) 291-4322
Executive search and consulting firm dedicated to placing professionals in part-time and project/consulting positions.

Families and Work Institute
330 Seventh Avenue
New York, NY 10001
(212) 465-2044
A nonprofit organization focusing on policy research and corporate strategic planning. Serves as a national clearinghouse for information on work/family–related issues and develops training programs and educational materials for government and business.

Family Resource Coalition
200 S. Michigan Avenue, Suite 1520
Chicago, IL 60604
(312) 341-0900
With more than 2,000 individuals and organizations as members, this organization produces numerous publications including work/family program resource kits for employers.

Family Service America
11700 West Lake Park Drive
Park Place
Milwaukee, WI 53224
(414) 359-1040
Provides referrals nationwide to individuals seeking work/family counseling.

Forty Plus Clubs
Provides job search assistance and referrals for people over forty. There are seventeen Forty-Plus organizations. Check the telephone directory for one in your area.

Gil Gordon Associates
10 Donner Court
Monmouth Junction, NJ 08852
(201) 329-2266
Provides telecommuting consulting services and publishes a regular newsletter devoted to telecommuting.

Hewitt Associates
100 Half Day Road
Lincolnshire, IL 60069
(708) 295-5000
Conducts research and designs programs on compensation and benefits for companies.

National Council for Research on Women
530 Broadway, 10th Floor
New York, NY 10012
(212) 274-0730
Provides research on women's issues.

National Council of Jewish Women
Center for the Child
53 W. 23rd Street
New York, NY 10010
(212) 645-4048
Conducts research on balancing work and family responsibilities.

New Ways to Work
785 Market Street, Suite 950
San Francisco, CA 94103
(415) 552-1000
A resource center that conducts research, serves as a clearinghouse for information on alternative work options, and promotes flexibility in the workplace.

Options, Inc.
225 S. 15th Street, Suite 1635
Philadelphia, PA 19102
(215) 735-2202
Provides consulting services to individuals and employers interested in flexible work arrangements.

Part-Time Resources
399 E. Putnam Avenue
Cos Cob, CT 06807
(203) 629-3255
A recruiting and consulting firm offering assistance in working part-time.

9 to 5
National Association of Working Women
614 Superior Avenue, NW
Cleveland, OH 44113
(216) 566-9308
A membership organization for office workers that operates a Job Survival
Hotline (1-800-522-0925). Trained job counselors respond to questions
about flexible jobs, maternity leave, and balancing work and family.

Professional Alternatives
601 Lakeshore Parkway, Suite 1050
Minnetonka, MN 55305
(612) 449-5189
Provides job counseling and placement for individuals interested in
flexible work arrangements.

U.S. Office of Personnel Management
Pay and Leave Administrator
1900 E Street, NW
Washington, D.C. 20415
(202) 606-2858
Provides information and research on flexible job programs within the
federal government.

Work/Family Directions, Inc.
930 Commonwealth Avenue West
Boston, MA 02215-1212
(617) 278-4000
A consulting firm whose services include research, strategic planning, and
nationwide child- and elder-care referrals.

Work Options Resource
P.O. Box 1011
Kaneohe, Hawaii 96744
(808) 948-2255
Consults with individuals and businesses interested in flexible work options.

APPENDIX C: FURTHER READINGS

General Resources

The Association of Part-Time Professionals. *Working Options*, Falls Church, VA: Association of Part-Time Professionals.

Belous, Richard S. *The Contingent Economy: The Growth of the Temporary, Part-Time and Subcontracted Workforce.* Washington, D.C.: National Planning Association, 1989.

Boyett, Joseph H., and Henry P. Conn. *Workplace 2000: The Revolution Reshaping American Business.* New York: Penguin Books, 1991.

Bureau of National Affairs. "Alternative Work Schedules: Changing Times for a Changing Workforce." *The National Report on Work and Family.* Special Report no. 5. Washington, D.C.: Buraff Publications, May 1988.

———. *BNA's Directory of Work and Family Programs.* Washington, D.C.: Bureau of National Affairs, 1991.

———. *Work and Family Today: 100 Key Statistics.* Special Report Series on Work and Family. Special Report no. 41. Washington, D.C.: Buraff Publications, May 1991.

Byalick, Marcia, and Linda Saslow. *The Three-Career Couple.* Princeton, N.J.: Peterson's, 1993.

Cardozo, Arlene R. *Sequencing.* New York: Atheneum, 1986.

Catalyst. *Flexible Work Arrangements: Establishing Options for Managers and Professionals.* New York: Catalyst, 1989.

Christensen, Kathleen E. *Flexible Staffing and Scheduling in U.S. Corporations.* Research Bulletin no. 240. New York: The Conference Board, 1989.

Clark, Charles S. "Work, Family and Stress." *CQ Researcher*, 14 August 1992.

The Conference Board. *Work-Family Roundtable: Flexibility.* New York: The Conference Board, December 1991.

Cook, Barbara Ensor. *A Mother's Choice: To Work or Not While Raising a Family.* White Hall, Va.: Betterway Publications, Inc., 1988.

Crane, Shena. *What Do I Do Now? Making Sense of Today's Changing Workplace.* Irvine, Calif.: Vista Press, 1993.

Deutschman, Alan. "Pioneers of the New Balance." *Fortune,* May 20, 1991.

Dynerman, Susan B., and Lynn O. Hayes. *The Best Jobs in America for Parents Who Want Careers—and Time for Children, Too.* New York: Ballantine Books, 1991.

Families and Work Institute. *An Evaluation of Johnson & Johnson's Work-Family Initiative.* New York, 1993.

———. *The Changing Workforce: Highlights and Sourcebook from the National Study.* New York, 1993.

Ferber, Marianne A., et al., eds. *Work and Family: Policies for a Changing Work Force.* Washington, D.C.: National Academy Press, 1991.

Ferguson, Trudi, and Joan S. Dunphy. *Answers to the Mommy Track: How Wives and Mothers in Business Reach the Top and Balance Their Lives.* Far Hills, N.J.: New Horizon Press, 1992.

Galinsky, Ellen. *Work and Family: 1992—Status Report and Outlook.* New York: Families and Work Institute, 1992.

Galinsky, Ellen, James T. Bond, and Dana E. Friedman. *The National Study of the Changing Workforce.* New York: Families and Work Institute, 1993.

Galinsky, Ellen, Dana E. Friedman, and Carol A. Hernandez. *The Corporate Reference Guide to Work-Family Programs.* New York: Families and Work Institute, 1991.

Hymowitz, Carol. "Trading Fat Paychecks for Free Time." *Wall Street Journal*, 5 August 1991.

Kiechel, Walter, III. "How We Will Work in the Year 2000." *Fortune*, May 17, 1993.

Killoughey, Donna M., ed. *Breaking Traditions: Work Alternatives for Lawyers*. Chicago: American Bar Association, 1993.

Lord, Michele, and Margaret King. *The State Reference Guide to Work-Family Programs for State Employees*. New York: Families and Work Institute, 1991.

Michaels, Bonnie, and Elizabeth McCarty. *Solving the Work/Family Dilemma Puzzle*. Homewood, Ill.: Business One Irwin, 1992.

Morgan, Hal, and Kerry Tucker. *Companies That Care: The Most Family-Friendly Companies in America—What They Offer and How They Got That Way*. New York: Simon and Schuster, 1991.

Moskowitz, Milton, and Carol Townsend. "100 Best Companies for Working Mothers: Eighth Annual Survey." *Working Mother*, October 1993.

Naisbitt, John, and Patricia Aburdeen. *Megatrends 2000*. New York: William Morrow & Co., 1990.

O'Hara, Bruce. *Put Work in Its Place: How to Redesign Your Job to Fit Your Life*. Victoria, British Columbia: Work Well Publications, 1988.

Olmsted, Barney, and Suzanne Smith. *Creating a Flexible Work Place: How to Select and Manage Alternative Work Options*. New York: AMACOM, 1988.

Prugh, Jeff. "The 10-Hour Days Can Be Tiring, but Employees Have the Perception of More Leisure Time as a Trade-Off." *Los Angeles Times*, 9 July 1993.

Saltzman, Amy. *Downshifting: Reinventing Success on a Slower Track*. New York: Harper Collins, 1991.

Shellenbarger, Susan. "Wall Street Journal Special Report: Work and Family." *Wall Street Journal*, 21 June 1993.

Schwartz, Felice N. *Breaking with Tradition: Women and Work—the New Facts of Life*. New York: Warner Books, 1992.

———. "Management Women and the New Facts of Life." *Harvard Business Review*, January/February 1989.

Swiss, Deborah J., and Judith P. Walker. *Women and the Work/Family*

Dilemma: How Today's Professional Women Are Finding Solutions.
New York: John Wiley & Sons, Inc., 1993.

Trost, Cathy. "To Cut Costs and Keep the Best People, More Concerns Offer Flexible Work Plans." *Wall Street Journal,* 18 February 1992.

U.S. Merit Systems Protection Board. *Balancing Work Responsibilities and Family Needs: The Federal Civil Service Response.* Washington, D.C.: U.S. Government Printing Office, 1991.

Vanderkolk, Barbara Schwarz, and Ardis Armstrong Young. *The Work and Family Revolution: How Companies Can Keep Employees Happy and Business Profitable.* New York: Facts on File, 1991.

"Women's Changing Role." Wylie, Texas: Information Plus, 1992.

"Work and Family." *Business Week,* June 28,1993.

"Workforce 2000, Competing in a Seller's Market: Is Corporate America Prepared?" The Hudson Institute and Towers Perrin, Washington, D.C., July 1990.

Part-Time

Bergsman, Steve. "Part-Time Professionals Make the Choice." *Personnel Administration,* September 1989.

Bernstein, Harry. "Many Part-Timers Must Trade Job Security for Flexibility." *Los Angeles Times,* 24 May 1988.

Callaghan, Polly, and Heidi Hartmann. *Contingent Work: A Chart Book on Part-Time Employment and Temporary Employment.* Washington, D.C.: Economic Policy Institute, 1991.

Canape, Charlene. *The Part-Time Solution: The New Strategy for Managing Your Career While Managing Motherhood.* New York: Harper & Row, 1990.

Catchpole, Terry. "Empowering Part-Time Workers." *Industry Week,* 16 March 1992.

Engdahl, Lora. "Part-Time Professional, Full-Time Commitment." *Executive Financial Woman,* Spring 1990.

Evans, Sandra. "More Fast-Track Professionals Are Braking for Families." *Washington Post*, 26 May 1992.

Hadley, Joyce. *Part-Time Careers: For Anyone Who Wants More Than Just a Job But Less Than a 40-Hour Week.* Hawthorne, N.J.: Career Press, 1993.

Levitan, Sar A., and Elizabeth A. Conway. "Part-Timers: Living on Half-Rations." *Challenge,* May/June 1988.

Loveman, Gary W. "The Case of the Part-Time Partner." *Harvard Business Review,* September/October 1990.

McHenry, Susan, and Linda Lee Small. "Does Part-Time Pay Off?" *Ms. Magazine,* March 1989.

"The Part-Time Solution: Here's How to Convince Management." *Working Mother,* August 1988.

Tilly, Chris. *Short Hours, Short Shift: Causes and Consequences of Part-Time Work.* Washington, D.C.: Economic Policy Institute, 1990.

Wise, Nicole. "Successful Strategies for Part-Time Work." *Parents Magazine,* December 1988.

"Working Part-Time Without Paying the Penalty." *New York Times,* 3 August 1990.

Job Sharing

Bahls, Jane Easter. "Two for One: A Working Idea." *Nation's Business,* June 1989.

"Employers Find Job-Sharing Programs Can Work: More Time, Less Stress Biggest Advantages." *Cincinnati Enquirer,* 13 July 1992.

Hoffman, Sharona. "Two Heads Are Better Than One." *School Food Service Journal,* March 1993.

Olmsted, Barney, and Suzanne Smith. *The Job Sharing Handbook.* Berkeley, Calif.: Ten Speed Press, 1983.

Saltzman, Amy. "One Job, Two Contented Workers." *U.S. News & World Report,* 14 November 1988.

Telecommuting

Anapol, Lynda, and Leslie Crawford. "Pioneering a New Workplace Option: Telecommuting and Pacific Bell." *Work Times,* Spring 1986.

Benham, Barbara Tzivanis. "Telecommuting: There's No Place Like Home." *Best's Review* (Life/Health), May 1988.

Fleming, Lis. *The One-Minute Commuter: How to Keep Your Job and Stay at Home Telecommuting.* Davis, Calif.: Fleming, Ltd., 1990.

Gil Gordon Associates. *Telecommuting Review: The Gordon Report.* Monmouth Junction, N.J.: Gil Gordon Associates.

Gordon, Gil E., and Marcia Kelly. *Telecommuting: How to Make It Work for You and Your Company.* Englewood Cliffs, N.J.: Prentice-Hall, 1986.

Heifetz, Laurel. *Final Focus Group Report: Puget Sound Telecommuting Demonstration.* Olympia, Wash.: Washington State Energy Office, 1992.

Meade, Jeff. *Home Sweet Office.* Princeton, N.J.: Peterson's, 1993.

Pratt, Joanne H. *Home Teleworking: A Study of Its Pioneers.* Technological Forecasting and Social Change, 1984.

Schaefer-Jacobs, Debbie. *Flexiplace: An Opportunity to Work at Home.* Four Star, Smithsonian Institution Women's Council, Summer 1992.

Schepp, Brad. *The Telecommuter's Handbook: How to Work for a Salary— Without Ever Leaving the House.* Pharos Books, 1990.

Segal, Edward. "Home Work." *Government Executive,* May 1991.

Employee Benefits

Berstein, Aaron. "Benefits Are Getting More Flexible." *Business Week,* September 8, 1986.

Hewitt Associates. *Survey of Benefits for Part-Time Employees.* Lincolnshire, Ill.: Hewitt Associates, 1991.

———. *Work and Family Benefits Provided by Major U.S. Employers in 1993.* Lincolnshire, Ill.: Hewitt Associates, 1993.

Luciano, Lani. "The Good News About Employee Benefits." *Money,* June 1992.

"A New Day for Worker Benefits." *Boston Globe,* 23 August 1988.

Nontraditional Benefits for the Workforce of 2000. Brookfield, Wis.: International Foundation of Employee Benefit Plans, August 1990.

"Part-Time Workers Are Ruled Eligible for Pension Benefits." *New York Times,* 5 June 1988.

Tober, Pamela A. "The Emerging Flexible Workplace." *Compensation and Benefits Review,* January/February 1988.

U.S. Bureau of Labor Statistics. "BLS Reports on Employee Benefits in Medium and Large Private Industry Establishments, 1991." Press release. December 9, 1992.

Consulting/ Homebased Work/ Temping

Ansberry, Clare. "Workers Are Forced to Take More Jobs with Few Benefits." *Wall Street Journal,* 11 March 1993.

Applegate, Jane. *Succeeding in Small Business—The 101 Toughest Problems and How to Solve Them.* New York: Penguin Books, 1992.

Arden, Lynie. *The Work-at-Home Sourcebook.* Boulder, Colo.: Live Oak Publications, 1992.

Black, Kathryn Stechert. "The New Professional Temporaries." *Working Mother,* November 1990.

Broudy, Eve. *Professional Temping: A Guide to Bridging Career Gaps.* New York: Collier Books, 1989.

Castro, Janice. "Disposable Workers." *Time,* March 29, 1993.

Dasch, Deborah A., and Martha I. Finney. "Filling In for Feds." *Government Temporaries,* May 1991.

Diesenhouse, Susan. "In a Shaky Economy, Even Professionals Are 'Temps.'" *New York Times,* 16 May 1993.

Edwards, Paul, and Sarah Edwards. *Working from Home: Everything You Need to Know about Living and Working under the Same Roof.* 3rd ed. Los Angeles, Calif.: Jeremy P. Tarcher, Inc., 1990.

Fehr, Stephen C. "Busy Suburbs Have a New Driving Force: Parents Hire Taxis to Shuttle Children." *Washington Post,* 15 August 1993.

Holz, Herman. *The Complete Work-at-Home Companion.* Rocklin, Calif.: Prima Publishing & Communications, 1990.

Justice, Peggy O'Connell. *The Temp Track: Make One of the Hottest Job Trends of the 90s Work for You.* Princeton, N.J.: Peterson's, 1994.

Mendenhall, Karen. *Making the Most of the Temporary Employment Market.* White Hall, Va: Betterway Publications, 1993.

Morrow, Lance. "The Temping of America." *Time,* March 29, 1993.

Careers/Job Search

Birsner, E. Patricia. *Mid-Career Job Hunting: Official Handbook of the Forty Plus Club*. New York: Simon & Schuster, 1991.

Bolles, Richard N. *What Color Is Your Parachute?* Berkeley, Calif.: Ten Speed Press, 1993.

Charland, William A., Jr. *Career Shifting: Starting Over in a Changing Economy*. Holbrook, Mass.: Bob Adams, Inc., 1993.

Connor, Robert J. *Cracking the Over-50 Job Market*. New York: Penguin Books, 1992.

Danna, Jo. *Starting Over: You in the New Workplace*. Briarwood, N.Y.: Palomino Press, 1990.

Kaplan, Robbie Miller. *The Whole Career Sourcebook*. New York: AMACOM, 1991.

Kleiman, Carol. *The 100 Best Jobs for the 1990s and Beyond*. Chicago: Dearborn Financial Publishing, Inc., 1992.

Krannich, Ronald L. *Careering and Re-careering for the 1990s*. Woodbridge, Va.: Impact Publications, 1991.

Otterbourg, Robert K. *It's Never Too Late: 150 Men and Women Who Changed Their Careers*. Hauppauge, N.Y.: Barron's, 1993.

NOTES

Chapter 1: In Pursuit of Flexibility

1. "Women's Changing Role," (Wylie, Texas: Information Plus, 1991), 58.
2. Charles S. Clark, "Work, Family and Stress," *CQ Researcher* (August 14, 1992), 691.
3. Carol Hymowitz, "Trading Fat Paychecks for Free Time," *Wall Street Journal* (August 5, 1991), B1.
4. Ellen Galinsky, James T. Bond, and Dana E. Friedman, *The National Study of the Changing Workforce* (New York: Families and Work Institute, 1993), 2.
5. Barbara Schwarz Vanderkolk and Ardis Armstrong Young, *The Work and Family Revolution: How Companies Can Keep Employees Happy and Business Profitable* (New York: Facts on File, 1991), 139.
6. Susan Bacon Dynerman and Lynn O'Rourke Hayes, *The Best Jobs in American for Parents Who Want Careers and Time for Children, Too.* (New York: Rawson Associates, 1991), 40.
7. Al Gore, *From Red Tape to Results: Creating a Government That Works Better & Costs Less* (Washington, D.C.: Government Printing Office, 1993).
8. *An Evaluation of Johnson & Johnson's Work-Family Initiative* (New York: Families and Work Institute, 1993), 9.
9. Ellen Galinsky, *Work and Family: 1992—Status Report and Outlook* (New York: Families and Work Institute, 1992), 1.
10. Armin A. Brott, "Values Collide on the 'Daddy Track,'" *Washington Post* (August 19, 1993), C5.

Chapter 2: New Ways to Work

1. The Association of Part-Time Professionals, *Working Options* (April 1993).
2. Kathleen Christensen, *Flexible Staffing and Scheduling in U.S. Corporations*, Research Bulletin No. 240 (New York: The Conference Board, 1989), 12.

3. International Foundation of Employee Benefit Plans, *Nontraditional Benefits for the Workforce of 2000* (Brookfield, Wis.: August 1990).
4. The Conference Board, *Work-Family Roundtable: Flexibility* (New York: December 1991).
5. Clark, "Work, Family and Stress," 706.
6. Stephen C. Fehr, "Moving the Job Closer to the Commuter," *Washington Post* (September 26, 1993).
7. Ibid.

Chapter 3: Fitting Flexibility into Your Career

1. Ronald L. Krannich, *Careering and Re-careering for the 1990s* (Woodbridge, Va.: Impact Publications, 1991), 3.
2. Amy Saltzman, *Downshifting: Reinventing Success on a Slower Track* (New York: Harper Collins, 1991), 17.
3. Ibid.
4. Ibid.
5. Trudi Ferguson and Joan S. Dunphy, *Answers to the Mommy Track: How Wives and Mothers in Business Reach the Top and Balance Their Lives* (Far Hills, N.J.: New Horizon Press, 1992), 58.
6. Deborah J. Swiss and Judith P. Walker, *Women and the Work/Family Dilemma: How Today's Professional Women Are Finding Solutions* (New York: John Wiley & Sons, Inc., 1993), 239.
7. Clark, "Work, Family and Stress," 702.
8. Brott, "Values Collide on the 'Daddy Track,'" C5.
9. Ibid.
10. Shari Rudavsky, "New Fathers Reluctant to Take Time Out," *Washington Post* (July 7, 1992).
11. Ibid.
12. Swiss and Walker, *Women and the Work/Family Dilemma,* 193.

Chapter 4: Fitting Flexibility into Your Budget

1. U.S. Bureau of Labor Statistics, "BLS Reports on Employee Benefits in Medium and Large Private Industry Establishments, 1991," press release, December 9, 1992.

2. Hewitt Associates, *Survey of Benefits for Part-Time Employees* (Lincolnshire, Ill.: 1991).

Chapter 5: Steps to Redesigning Your Job

1. Catalyst, *Flexible Work Arrangements: Establishing Options for Managers and Professionals* (New York: 1989).
2. The Conference Board, *Work-Family Roundtable*.
3. Chuck Hawkins, "Work and Family," *Business Week* (June 28, 1993), 88.
4. Catalyst, *Flexible Work Arrangements*.

Chapter 9: Finding a New Flexible Job

1. Lois Angelowitz Anzelowitz, ed., "The 25 Hottest Careers," *Working Woman* (July 1993).
2. Ellyn E. Spragins, ed., "Managing People," *Inc.* (November 1992), 36.
3. Joyce Hadley, *Part-Time Careers: For Anyone Who Wants More Than Just a Job But Less Than a 40-Hour Week* (Hawthorne, N.J.: Career Press, 1993), 38.
4. Carol Kleiman, *The 100 Best Jobs for the 1990s and Beyond* (Chicago: Dearborn Financial Publishing, Inc., 1992).

Chapter 10: Other Career Tracks

1. Stephen C. Fehr, "Busy Suburbs Have a New Driving Force: Parents Hire Taxis to Shuttle Children," *Washington Post* (August 15, 1993), A1.
2. Peggy O'Connell Justice, *The Temp Track: Make One of the Hottest Job Trends of the 90s Work for You* (Princeton, N.J.: Peterson's, 1994), 11.
3. Ibid., 158.

INDEX